SCOTTISH STATUTORY INSTRUMENTS

2018 No. 66

NATIONAL HEALTH SERVICE

The National Health Service (General Medical Services Contracts) (Scotland) Regulations 2018

Made	15th February 2018
Laid before the Scottish Parliament	19th February 2018

Coming into force in accordance with regulation 1

CONTENTS

PART 1
GENERAL

1. Citation and commencement
2. Application
3. Interpretation

PART 2
CONTRACTORS

4. Conditions: general
5. Conditions relating solely to medical practitioners
6. General conditions relating to all contracts
7. Further conditions relating to all contracts
8. Reasons
9. Appeal
10. Continuing conditions relating to contracts
11. Continuing conditions relating to contracts – sufficient involvement in patient care

PART 3
PRE-CONTRACT DISPUTE RESOLUTION

12. Pre-contract disputes

PART 4
HEALTH SERVICE BODY STATUS

13. Health service body status

PART 5
CONTRACTS: MANDATORY TERMS

14. Parties to the contract
15. NHS contracts
16. Contracts with a partnership
17. Duration
18. Essential services
19. Additional services
20. Opt outs of additional services
21. Services generally
22. Services generally
23. Services generally
24. Additional obligations in relation to practice premises
25. Certificates
26. Finance
27. Finance
28. Fees and charges
29. Arrangements on termination
30. Other contractual terms
31. Implied contract terms

PART 6
FUNCTIONS OF AREA MEDICAL COMMITTEE

32. Functions of area medical committee

PART 7
TRANSITIONAL PROVISIONS

33. Out of hours

PART 8
SUPPLEMENTARY

34. Revocations
35. Consequential amendments

SCHEDULE 1 — ADDITIONAL SERVICES
SCHEDULE 2 — OPT OUTS OF ADDITIONAL SERVICES
SCHEDULE 3 — MINIMUM STANDARDS FOR PRACTICE PREMISES
SCHEDULE 4 — LIST OF PRESCRIBED MEDICAL CERTIFICATES
SCHEDULE 5 — FEES AND CHARGES
SCHEDULE 6 — OTHER CONTRACTUAL TERMS
    PART 1 — PROVISION OF SERVICES
    PART 2 — PATIENTS
    PART 3 — PRESCRIBING AND DISPENSING

PART 4 — PERSONS WHO PERFORM SERVICES
PART 5 — DATA PROTECTION, RECORDS, INFORMATION, NOTIFICATIONS AND RIGHTS OF ENTRY
PART 6 — COMPLAINTS
PART 7 — DISPUTE RESOLUTION
PART 8 — VARIATION AND TERMINATION OF CONTRACTS
PART 9 — MISCELLANEOUS
PART 10 — QUALITY
SCHEDULE 7 — CLOSURE NOTICE
SCHEDULE 8 — INFORMATION TO BE INCLUDED IN PRACTICE LEAFLETS
SCHEDULE 9 — REVOCATIONS
SCHEDULE 10 — CONSEQUENTIAL AMENDMENTS

The Scottish Ministers make the following Regulations, in exercise of the powers conferred by sections 9(6), 17A(6), 17K, 17L, 17N, 17O, 28(1), 105(7) and 106(a) of the National Health Service (Scotland) Act 1978(a) and all other powers enabling them to do so.

PART 1

GENERAL

Citation and commencement

1.—(1) These Regulations may be cited as the National Health Service (General Medical Services Contracts) (Scotland) Regulations 2018.

(2) Subject to paragraph (3), these Regulations come into force on 1st April 2018.

(3) Paragraph 64(2) of Schedule 6 comes into force on 25th May 2018.

Application

2. These Regulations apply to a contract—

(a) to which the National Health Service (General Medical Services Contracts) (Scotland) Regulations 2004(b) applied immediately before 1st April 2018; or

(b) which is entered into between a contractor and the Health Board on or after 1st April 2018.

(a) 1978 c.29. Section 17A was inserted by section 30 of the National Health Service and Community Care Act 1990 (c.19) ("the 1990 Act"). Section 17A was moved under a new heading entitled "NHS Contracts" by section 31 of the National Health Service (Primary Care) Act 1997 (c.46). Sections 17K, 17N and 17O were inserted by section 4 of the Primary Medical Services (Scotland) Act 2004 (asp 1) ("the 2004 Act"). Section 17L was substituted by section 39(1) of the Tobacco and Primary Medical Services (Scotland) Act 2010 (asp 3). Section 28(1) was relevantly amended by section 3(4) of the National Health Service (Amendment) Act 1986 (c.66) and by paragraph 1(8) of schedule 4 of the 2004 Act. Section 105(7) was amended by paragraph 5 of schedule 6 and schedule 7 of the Health Services Act 1980 (c.53), paragraph 24 of schedule 9 of the Health and Social Services and Social Security Adjudications Act 1983 (c.41) and paragraph 60 of schedule 4 of the Health Act 1999 (c.8). Section 108(1) contains a definition of "prescribed" and "regulations" relevant to the statutory powers under which these Regulations are made. The functions of the Secretary of State were transferred to the Scottish Ministers by virtue of section 53 of the Scotland Act 1998 (c.46).
(b) S.S.I. 2004/115, as amended by paragraph 18 of schedule 4 of the Charities and Trustee Investment (Scotland) Act 2005 (asp 10), and by S.S.I. 2004/142, S.S.I. 2004/162, S.S.I. 2004/163, S.S.I. 2004/215, S.S.I. 2005/337, S.S.I. 2006/247, S.S.I. 2007/206, S.S.I. 2007/392, S.S.I. 2007/501, S.S.I. 2009/183, S.I. 2010/231, S.I. 2010/234, S.S.I. 2010/93, S.S.I. 2010/394, S.S.I. 2011/32, S.S.I. 2011/55, S.S.I. 2011/211, S.S.I. 2012/9, S.S.I. 2012/36, S.I. 2012/1479, S.I. 2012/1916, S.I. 2013/235, S.S.I. 2014/73, S.S.I. 2014/148, S.I. 2014/1887, S.S.I. 2016/393 and S.I. 2016/696.

Interpretation

3.—(1) In these Regulations—

"the Act" means the National Health Service (Scotland) Act 1978;

"the 1998 Act" means the Data Protection Act 1998(**a**);

"the 2004 Act" means the Primary Medical Services (Scotland) Act 2004(**b**);

"the 2004 Regulations" means the National Health Service (General Medical Services Contracts) (Scotland) Regulations 2004;

"the 2010 Order" means the Postgraduate Medical Education and Training Order of Council 2010(**c**);

"additional services" means one or more of—

(a) cervical screening services;

(b) contraceptive services;

(c) vaccinations and immunisations;

(d) childhood vaccinations and immunisations;

(e) child health surveillance services; and

(f) maternity medical services;

"adjudicator" means the Scottish Ministers or a panel of 3 persons appointed by the Scottish Ministers (as the case may be) under paragraph 91 of schedule 6;

"advanced electronic signature" means an advanced electronic signature within the meaning given in Article 3(11) of Regulation (EU) No 910/2014 of the European Parliament and of the Council of 23rd July 2014 on electronic identification and trust services for electronic transactions in the internal market(**d**) and repealing Directive 1993/93/EC;

"appliance" means an appliance which is included in a list for the time being approved by the Scottish Ministers for the purposes of section 27(1) of the Act(**e**);

"area medical committee" means the committee of that name recognised under section 9 of the Act(**f**) (local consultative committees) in the area of the Health Board;

"area pharmaceutical committee" means the committee of that name recognised under section 9 of the Act (local consultative committees) in the area of the Health Board;

"assessment panel" means a committee or subcommittee of a Health Board ("the first Health Board") (other than the Health Board ("the second Health Board") which is a party or prospective party to the contract in question) appointed by the first Health Board at the request of the second Health Board to exercise functions under paragraph 2 or 3 of schedule 2 or paragraph 28, 32, or 37 of schedule 6 and which must consist of—

(a) the Chief Executive of the first Health Board or an Executive Director of that Health Board nominated by that Chief Executive;

(b) a person representative of patients in an area other than that of the second Health Board; and

---

(**a**) 1998 c.29.
(**b**) 2004 asp 1.
(**c**) S.I. 2010/473.
(**d**) OJ L 257, 28.8.2014, p.73. Article 3(11) provides that an "advanced electronic signature" means an electronic signature which meets the requirements set out in Article 26 of that instrument. The requirements in Article 26 are that the electronic signature is (a) uniquely linked to the signatory; (b) capable of identifying the signatory; (c) created using electronic signature creation data that the signatory can, with a high level of confidence, use under his sole control; and (d) linked to the data signed therewith in such a way that any subsequent change in the data is detectable.
(**e**) Section 27(1) was amended by section 20 of the Health Services Act 1980, paragraph 19 of the National Health Service and Community Care Act 1990 ("the 1990 Act"), section 3 of the Medicinal Products: Prescription by Nurses etc. Act 1992 (c.28), paragraph 44 of schedule 2 of the National Health Service (Primary Care) Act 1997 and section 44 of the Health and Social Care Act 2001 (c.15).
(**f**) Section 9 was amended by section 29(5) of the 1990 Act and paragraph 43 of the Health Act 1999.

(c) a person representative of the area medical committee which does not represent practitioners in the area of the second Health Board;

"care home service" has the same meaning as in paragraph 2 of schedule 12 of the Public Services Reform (Scotland) Act 2010(**a**);

"CCT" means a Certificate of Completion of Training awarded under section 34L(1) of the Medical Act 1983(**b**), including any such certificate awarded in pursuance of the competent authority functions of the General Medical Council specified in section 49B and schedule 4A of that Act(**c**);

"cervical screening services" means the services described in paragraph 2(2) of schedule 1;

"charity trustee" means one of the persons having the general control and management of the administration of a charity;

"child" means a person who has not attained the age of 16 years;

"child health surveillance services" means the services described in paragraph 6(2) of schedule 1;

"childhood vaccinations and immunisations" means the services described in paragraph 5(2) of schedule 1;

"clinical commissioning group" means a body established under section 14D of the National Health Service Act 2006(**d**);

"closed" in relation to the contractor's list of patients, means closed to applications for inclusion in the list of patients other than from immediate family members of registered patients;

"conditional disqualification" has the same meaning as in section 29C(1) of the Act(**e**) and includes a decision under provisions in force in England, Wales or Northern Ireland corresponding (whether or not exactly) to a conditional disqualification;

"contraceptive services" means the services described in paragraph 3(2) of schedule 1;

"contract" means, except where the context otherwise requires, a general medical services contract under section 17J of the Act(**f**) (Health Boards' power to enter into general medical services contracts);

"contractor" means a person with whom a Health Board enters into a contract;

"contractor's list of patients" means the list prepared and maintained by a Health Board under paragraph 11 of schedule 6;

"core hours" means the period beginning at 0800 hours and ending at 1830 hours on any working day;

"dispensing services" means the provision of drugs, medicines and appliances;

"disqualified" means, unless the context otherwise requires, disqualified by the Tribunal (or a corresponding decision under provisions in force in England, Wales or Northern Ireland corresponding, whether or not exactly, to disqualified), but does not include conditional disqualification, and "disqualification" is to be construed accordingly;

"Drug Tariff" means the statement published under regulation 12 (payments to pharmacy contractors and standards of drugs and appliances) of the Pharmaceutical Regulations;

"electronic communication" has the same meaning as in section 15 of the Electronic Communications Act 2000(**g**);

(**a**) 2010 asp 8.
(**b**) 1983 c.54. Section 34 was inserted by S.I. 2010/234.
(**c**) Section 49B was inserted by S.I. 2007/3101 and was amended by S.I. 2008/1774 and S.I. 2010/234. Schedule 4A was inserted by S.I. 2007/3101 and was amended by S.I. 2010/234 and S.I. 2016/1030.
(**d**) 2006 c.41. Section 14D was inserted by section 25(1) of the Health and Social Care Act 2012 (c.7).
(**e**) Section 29C(1) was inserted by section 58 of the Health Act 1999. There are amendments to section 29C not relevant to these Regulations.
(**f**) Section 17J was inserted by section 4 of the Primary Medical Services (Scotland) Act 2004.
(**g**) 2000 c.7. Section 15 was amended by paragraph 158 of schedule 17 of the Communications Act 2003 (c.21).

"electronic prescription form" means a prescription form as defined in paragraph (b) of the definition of "prescription form";

"electronic signature" has the meaning attributed to it in section 7(2)(a) of the Electronic Communications Act 2000;

"enhanced services" are—

(a) services other than essential services or additional services; or

(b) essential services or additional services or an element of such a service that a contractor agrees under the contract to provide in accordance with specifications set out in a plan, which requires of the contractor an enhanced level of service provision compared to that which it needs generally to provide in relation to that service or element of service;

"ePharmacy service" means the electronic system provided by the Agency by which electronic prescription forms are transmitted;

"essential services" means the services required to be provided in accordance with regulation 18;

"GDPR" means Regulation (EU) 2016/679 of the European Parliament and of the Council of 27th April 2016 on the protection of natural persons with regard to the processing of personal data and on the free movement of such data(**b**), and repealing Directive 95/46/EC;

"general medical practitioner" means, unless the context otherwise requires, a medical practitioner whose name is included in the General Practitioner Register kept by the General Medical Council;

"global sum" has the meaning given to it in the GMS Statement of Financial Entitlements;

"GMS Statement of Financial Entitlements" means the directions given by the Scottish Ministers under section 17M of the Act(**c**) (payments by Health Boards under general medical services contracts);

"GP Registrar" means a medical practitioner who is being trained in general practice by a general medical practitioner who is approved under section 34I(**d**) of the Medical Act 1983 for the purpose of providing training under that section, whether as part of training leading to a CCT or otherwise;

"Health and Social Care trust" means a Health and Social Care trust established under Article 10(1) of the Health and Personal Social Services (Northern Ireland) Order 1991(**e**) and renamed by section 1(3) of the Health and Social Care (Reform) Act (Northern Ireland) 2009(**f**);

"Health Board" means, unless the context otherwise requires, the Health Board which is a party, or prospective party, to a contract;

"health care professional" has the same meaning as in section 17L(8) of the Act and "health care profession" is to be construed accordingly;

"health service body" means any person or body referred to in section 17A(2) of the Act (NHS contracts)(**g**) and includes, except where otherwise expressly provided, any person who is to be regarded as a health service body in accordance with regulation 13;

(**a**) Section 7(2) was amended by S.I. 2016/696.
(**b**) OJ L 119, 4.5.2016, p.1–88.
(**c**) Section 17M was inserted by section 4 of the Primary Medical Services (Scotland) Act 2004. Directions are normally given before the beginning of the financial year to which they are to apply and will be available on http://www.show.scot.nhs.uk.
(**d**) Section 34I was inserted by S.I. 2010/234.
(**e**) S.I. 1991/194 (N.I.1). Article 10 was amended by S.I. 1994/429 (N.I. 2), sections 43 and 44 of the Health and Personal Services Act (Northern Ireland) 2001 (c.3) and paragraph 1 of schedule 6 of the Health and Social Care (Reform) Act (Northern Ireland) 2009 (c.1).
(**f**) 2009 c.1.
(**g**) Section 17A(2) was inserted by section 30 of the National Health Service and Community Care Act 1990 and was amended by paragraph 36 of schedule 2 of the National Health Service (Primary Care) Act 1997, paragraph 46 of schedule 4 and paragraph 1 of schedule 5 of the Health Act 1999, paragraph 1 of schedule 14 of the Health and Social Care (Community Health and Standards) Act 2003 (c.43), paragraph 8 of schedule 17 of the Public Services Reform (Scotland) Act 2010 and paragraph 2 of schedule 21 of the Health and Social Care Act 2012.

"immediate family member" means—

(a) a spouse or civil partner;

(b) a person whose relationship with the registered patient has the characteristics of the relationship between spouses or civil partners;

(c) a parent or step-parent;

(d) a son;

(e) a daughter;

(f) a child of whom the registered patient is—

    (i) the guardian; or

    (ii) the carer duly authorised by the local authority to whose care the child has been committed under the Children (Scotland) Act 1995(**a**); or

(g) a grandparent;

"independent nurse prescriber" means a person—

(a) who is either engaged or employed by the contractor, or where the contractor is a partnership, is a partner in that partnership; and

(b) who is registered in the Nursing and Midwifery Register; and

(c) against whose name is recorded in that register an annotation signifying that they are qualified to order drugs, medicines and appliances as a community practitioner nurse prescriber, a nurse independent prescriber or a nurse independent/supplementary prescriber;

"independent prescriber" means—

(a) an independent nurse prescriber;

(b) a pharmacist independent prescriber;

(c) a physiotherapist independent prescriber;

(d) a podiatrist or chiropodist prescriber;

(e) a therapeutic radiographer independent prescriber; or

(f) a paramedic independent prescriber;

"licensing authority" is to be construed in accordance with regulation 6(2) of the Human Medicines Regulations 2012(**b**);

"licensing body" means any body that licenses or regulates any profession;

"limited liability partnership" means a limited liability partnership incorporated in accordance with section 2 of the Limited Liability Partnerships Act 2000(**c**);

"limited partnership" means a partnership registered in accordance with section 5 of the Limited Partnerships Act 1907(**d**);

"list" has, unless the context otherwise requires, the meaning assigned to it in section 29(8) of the Act(**e**) and includes a list corresponding to such a list in England, Wales or Northern Ireland;

"local dispute resolution process" means the process for encouraging local resolution of disputes specified in paragraph 89 of schedule 6;

(**a**) 1995 c.36.
(**b**) S.I. 2012/1916.
(**c**) 2000 c.12. Section 2 was amended by S.I. 2009/1804 and S.I. 2016/340.
(**d**) 1907 c.24. Section 5 was amended by S.I. 2009/1940.
(**e**) Section 29 was substituted by section 58(1) of the Health Act 1999. Section 29 was further amended by paragraph 2(4) of schedule 2 of the Community Care and Health (Scotland) Act 2002 (asp 5), section 5(3) of the Primary Medical Services (Scotland) Act 2004 and section 26(2) and paragraph 2 of schedule 2 of the Smoking, Health and Social Care (Scotland) Act 2005 (asp 13).

"Local Health Board" means a body established under section 11 of the National Health Service (Wales) Act 2006(**a**);

"maternity medical services" means the services described in paragraph 7(1) of schedule 1;

"Medical Register" means the registers kept under section 2 of the Medical Act 1983(**b**);

"NHS contract" means a contract—

(a) which is a general medical services contract under section 17J of the Act; and

(b) which is a NHS contract within the meaning of section 17A(3) of the Act(**c**) as a consequence of which the contractor is being regarded as a health service body pursuant to regulation 13(1) or (4);

"NHS dispute resolution procedure" means the procedure for the resolution of disputes specified in paragraphs 91 and 92 of schedule 6;

"NHS foundation trust" has the same meaning as in section 30 of the National Health Service Act 2006(**d**);

"NHS trust" means a National Health Service trust established under section 25 of the National Health Service Act 2006;

"non-electronic prescription form" means a prescription form as defined in paragraph (a) of the definition of "prescription form";

"normal hours" means those days and hours on which and the times at which services under the contract are normally made available and may be different for different services;

"Nursing and Midwifery Register" means the register maintained by the Nursing and Midwifery Council under the Nursing and Midwifery Order 2001(**e**);

"open", in relation to the contractor's list of patients, means open to applications from patients in accordance with paragraph 12 of schedule 6;

"paramedic independent prescriber" means a person registered in Part 8 of the register maintained under article 5 of the Health and Social Work Professions Order 2001(**f**) and against whose name in that register is recorded an annotation signifying that the person is qualified to order drugs, medicines and appliances as a paramedic independent prescriber;

"parent" includes, in relation to any child, any adult who, in the opinion of the contractor, is for the time being discharging in respect of that child the obligations normally attaching to a parent in respect of a child;

"patient" means—

(a) a registered patient;

(b) a temporary resident;

(c) persons to whom the contractor is required to provide immediately necessary treatment under regulation 18(6) or (8) respectively; and

(d) any other person to whom the contractor has agreed to provide services under the contract;

"the Pharmaceutical Regulations" means the National Health Service (Pharmaceutical Services) (Scotland) Regulations 2009(**g**);

(**a**) 2006 c.42.
(**b**) Section 2 was amended by S.I. 2002/3135, S.I. 2006/1914, S.I. 2007/3103, S.I. 2008/1774 and S.I. 2014/1101.
(**c**) Section 17A(3) was inserted by section 30 of the National Health Service and Community Care Act 1990 and amended by paragraph 46 of schedule 4 and paragraph 1 of schedule 5 of the Health Act 1999.
(**d**) Section 30 was amended by section 159 of the Health and Social Care Act 2012.
(**e**) S.I. 2002/253.
(**f**) S.I. 2002/254, as retitled by section 213(6) of the Health and Social Care Act 2012. Article 5 was amended by S.I. 2009/1182. The title of this Order is the Health and Social Work Professions Order 2002 but is cited as the Health and Social Work Professions Order 2001 in accordance with section 213(4) of the Health and Social Care Act 2012.
(**g**) S.S.I. 2009/183.

"pharmacist" means a person who is registered as a pharmacist in—

(a) Part 1 or Part 4 of the register maintained under article 19 of the Pharmacy Order 2010(**a**); or

(b) the register maintained in pursuance of Articles 6 and 9 of the Pharmacy (Northern Ireland) Order 1976(**b**);

"pharmacist independent prescriber" means a pharmacist against whose name in the relevant register is recorded an annotation signifying that the pharmacist is qualified to order drugs, medicines and appliances as a pharmacist independent prescriber;

"physiotherapist independent prescriber" means a physiotherapist who is registered in Part 9 of the register maintained under article 5 of the Health and Social Work Professions Order 2001, and against whose name in that register is recorded an annotation signifying that the physiotherapist is qualified to order drugs, medicines and appliances as a physiotherapist independent prescriber;

"podiatrist or chiropodist independent prescriber" means a podiatrist or chiropodist who is registered in Part 2 of the register maintained under article 5 of the Health and Social Work Professions Order 2001, and against whose name in that register is recorded an annotation signifying that the podiatrist or chiropodist is qualified to order drugs, medicines and appliances as a podiatrist or chiropodist independent prescriber;

"practice" means the business operated by the contractor for the purpose of delivering services under the contract;

"practice area" means the area referred to in regulation 21(1)(d);

"practice leaflet" means a leaflet drawn up in accordance with paragraph 74 of schedule 6;

"practice premises" means an address specified in the contract as one at which services are to be provided under the contract;

"prescriber" means—

(a) a medical practitioner;

(b) an independent nurse prescriber;

(c) a supplementary prescriber;

(d) a pharmacist independent prescriber;

(e) a physiotherapist independent prescriber;

(f) a podiatrist or chiropodist independent prescriber;

(g) a therapeutic radiographer independent prescriber; and

(h) a paramedic independent prescriber,

who is either engaged or employed by the contractor or, where the contractor is a partnership, is a partner in that partnership;

"prescription form" means—

(a) a form provided by the Health Board and issued by a prescriber; or

(b) data that are created in an electronic form and which are signed with a prescriber's advanced electronic signature and transmitted as an electronic communication through the ePharmacy service,

to enable a person to obtain pharmaceutical services.

"prescription only medicine" means a medicine referred to in regulation 5(3) (classification of medicinal products) of the Human Medicines Regulations 2012;

(**a**) S.I. 2010/231.
(**b**) S.I. 1976/1213 (N.I. 22), as relevantly amended by S.R. (NI) 2008 No 192.

"primary medical services performers list" means the list of primary medical services performers prepared in accordance with regulations made under section 17P of the Act(**a**) (persons performing primary medical services);

"public or local holiday" means any public or local holiday which is agreed in writing between the Health Board and the contractor and which must, in aggregate, be no less than those available to NHS employees employed by the Health Board;

"Regional Health and Social Care Board" means the Regional Health and Social Care Board established under section 7 of the Health and Social Care (Reform) Act (Northern Ireland) 2009;

"registered patient" means—

(a) a person who is recorded by the Health Board as being on the contractor's list of patients; or

(b) a person whom the contractor has accepted for inclusion on its list of patients, whether or not notification of that acceptance has been received by the Health Board, and who has not been notified by the Health Board as having ceased to be on that list;

"relevant register" means—

(a) in relation to a nurse, the Nursing and Midwifery Register;

(b) in relation to a pharmacist—

   (i) Part 1 of the register maintained under article 19 of the Pharmacy Order 2010; or

   (ii) the register maintained in pursuance of Articles 6 and 9 of the Pharmacy (Northern Ireland) Order 1976; and

(c) in relation to a chiropodist and podiatrist, a physiotherapist, paramedic and a therapeutic radiographer, the relevant part of the register maintained by the Health Professions Council in pursuance of article 5 of the Health and Social Work Professions Order 2001;

"restricted availability appliance" means an appliance which is approved for particular categories of persons or particular purposes only;

"Scheduled drug" means—

(a) a drug, medicine or other substance specified in any directions given by the Scottish Ministers under section 17N(6) of the Act(**b**) as being a drug, medicine or other substance which may not be ordered for patients in the provision of medical services under the contract; or

(b) except where the conditions in paragraphs 40(2) and 41(2) of schedule 6 are satisfied, a drug, medicine or other substance which is specified in any directions given by the Scottish Ministers under section 17N(6) of the Act, as being a drug, medicine or other substance which can only be ordered for specified patients and specified purposes;

"section 17C provider" means a person or body who is providing primary medical services in accordance with an agreement pursuant to section 17C of the Act(**c**);

"supplementary prescriber" means a person who is either engaged or employed by the contractor, or where the contractor is a partnership, is a partner in that partnership, and whose name is registered in—

(a) the Nursing and Midwifery Register;

(b) Part 1 of the register maintained under article 19 of the Pharmacy Order 2010;

(c) the register maintained in pursuance of Articles 6 and 9 of the Pharmacy (Northern Ireland) Order 1976;

(**a**) Section 17P was inserted by section 5(2) of the Primary Medical Services (Scotland) Act 2004 ("the 2004 Act") (asp 1).
(**b**) Section 17N was inserted by section 4 of the 2004 Act.
(**c**) Section 17C was inserted by section 21(2) of the National Health Service (Primary Care) Act 1997 (c.46) and was amended by section 2(2) of the 2004 Act and paragraph 3 of schedule 21 of the Health and Social Care Act 2012 (c.7).

(d) the part of the register maintained by the Health Professions Council in pursuance of article 5 of the Health and Social Work Professions Order 2001 relating to—

  (i) chiropodists and podiatrists;

  (ii) physiotherapists;

  (iii) diagnostic or therapeutic radiographers;

  (iv) dietitians;

  (v) paramedics; or

(e) the register of optometrists maintained by the General Optical Council in pursuance of section 7 of the Opticians Act 1989(**a**),

and against whose name is recorded in the relevant register an annotation signifying that they are qualified to order drugs, medicines and appliances as a supplementary prescriber or, in the case of the Nursing and Midwifery Register, a nurse independent/supplementary prescriber;

"temporary resident" means a person accepted by the contractor as a temporary resident under paragraph 13 of schedule 6 and for whom the contractor's responsibility has not been terminated in accordance with that paragraph;

"therapeutic radiographer independent prescriber" means a person—

(a) registered in Part 11 of the register maintained under article 5 of the Health and Social Work Professions Order 2001; and

(b) against whose name in that register is recorded—

  (i) an entitlement to use the title "therapeutic radiographer"; and

  (ii) an annotation signifying that the person is qualified to order drugs, medicines and appliances as a therapeutic radiographer independent prescriber;

"the Tribunal" has the meaning indicated in section 29 of the Act (the NHS Tribunal);

"vaccinations and immunisations" means the services described in paragraph 4(2) of schedule 1;

"working day" means any day apart from Saturday, Sunday, Christmas Day, New Year's Day and any other public or local holiday; and

"writing" includes, unless otherwise expressly provided, transmission by electronic means and "written" is to be construed accordingly.

(2) In these Regulations, the use of the term "it" in relation to—

(a) the adjudicator is deemed to refer either to the Scottish Ministers or to the panel of 3 persons appointed by them, as the case may be; and

(b) a contractor is deemed to include a reference to a contractor who is an individual medical practitioner,

and related expressions are to be construed accordingly.

(3) Any reference in these Regulations to a numbered regulation or schedule or to a numbered paragraph of such a regulation or schedule is, unless otherwise expressly provided, a reference to a regulation or schedule bearing that number in these Regulations or, as the case may be, to a paragraph bearing that number in such a regulation or schedule.

(**a**) 1989 c.44. Section 7 was amended by S.I. 2005/848.

PART 2

CONTRACTORS

Conditions: general

4. A Health Board may only enter into a contract if the conditions set out in regulations 5, 6 and 7 are met.

Conditions relating solely to medical practitioners

5.—(1) In the case of a contract to be entered into with a medical practitioner, that practitioner must be a general medical practitioner who satisfies the conditions in regulations 6 and 7.

(2) In the case of a contract to be entered into with a partnership—

(a) at least one partner (who must not be a limited partner) must be a general medical practitioner;

(b) all the other partners must be individuals; and

(c) all the partners must satisfy the conditions in regulations 6 and 7.

(3) In the case of a contract to be entered into with a limited liability partnership—

(a) at least one member must be a general medical practitioner;

(b) all the other members must be individuals; and

(c) all the members must satisfy the conditions in regulations 6 and 7.

(4) In the case of a contract to be entered into with a company—

(a) at least one member of the company must be a general medical practitioner;

(b) all other members must be individuals;

(c) all the members must satisfy the conditions in regulations 6 and 7; and

(d) any director or secretary of the company must satisfy the conditions in regulation 6.

(5) In paragraphs (1), (2)(a), (3)(a) and (4)(a), "general medical practitioner" does not include a medical practitioner whose name is included in the General Practitioner Register by virtue of—

(a) article 4(3) of the 2010 Order (general practitioners eligible for entry in the General Practitioner Register) because of an exemption under regulation 5(1)(d) of one of the sets of Regulations specified in paragraph (6);

(b) article 6(2) of the 2010 Order (persons with acquired rights) by virtue of being a restricted service principal (within the meaning of one or more of the sets of Regulations specified in paragraph (7)) included in a list specified in that article; or

(c) article 6(6) of the 2010 Order.

(6) The regulations referred to in paragraph (5)(a) are the National Health Service (Vocational Training for General Medical Practice) (Scotland) Regulations 1998(**a**), the National Health Service (Vocational Training for General Medical Practice) Regulations 1997(**b**) and the Medical Practitioners (Vocational Training) Regulations (Northern Ireland) 1998(**c**).

(7) The regulations referred to in paragraph (5)(b) are the National Health Service (General Medical Services) Regulations 1992(**d**), the National Health Service (General Medical Services) (Scotland) Regulations 1995(**e**) and the General Medical Services Regulations (Northern Ireland) 1997(**f**).

(**a**) S.I. 1998/5. Those Regulations were revoked by S.I. 2003/1250.
(**b**) S.I. 1997/2817. Those Regulations were revoked by S.I. 2003/1250.
(**c**) S.R. (N.I.) 1998/No. 13. Those Regulations were revoked by S.I. 2003/1250.
(**d**) S.I. 1992/635. Those Regulations were revoked in respect of Wales by S.I. 2004/1016 (W. 113) and in respect of England by S.I. 2004/865.
(**e**) S.I. 1995/416. Those Regulations were revoked by S.S.I. 2004/114.
(**f**) S.R. (N.I.) 1997/No. 380. Those Regulations were revoked by S.R. (N.I.) 2004/No. 156.

General conditions relating to all contracts

6.—(1) It is a condition in the case of a contract to be entered into—

(a) with a medical practitioner, that the medical practitioner;

(b) with a partnership, that any member of the partnership or the partnership;

(c) with a limited liability partnership, that any member of the limited liability partnership or the limited liability partnership; and

(d) with a company, that—

   (i) the company;

   (ii) any member of the company;

   (iii) any director or secretary of the company,

must not fall within paragraph (2).

(2) A person falls within this paragraph if—

(a) the person has been disqualified or suspended by direction of the Tribunal made pursuant to section 32A(2) (applications for interim suspension) or 32B(1) (suspension pending appeal) of the Act(**a**), or under any provisions in force in England, Wales or Northern Ireland corresponding thereto;

(b) subject to paragraph (3), the person is disqualified or suspended (otherwise than by an interim suspension order or direction pending an investigation) from practising by any licensing body anywhere in the world;

(c) within the period of 5 years prior to the signing of the contract or commencement of the contract, whichever is the earlier, the person has been dismissed (otherwise than by reason of redundancy) from any employment by a health service body, unless—

   (i) the person has subsequently been employed by that health service body or another health service body and, where the person has been employed as a member of a health care profession, any subsequent employment has also been as a member of that profession; or

   (ii) that dismissal was the subject of a finding of unfair dismissal by any competently established tribunal or court;

(d) within the period of 5 years prior to signing the contract or commencement of the contract, whichever is the earlier, the person has been disqualified from a list anywhere in the United Kingdom unless the person's name has subsequently been included in such a list;

(e) the person has been convicted in the United Kingdom of—

   (i) murder; or

   (ii) a criminal offence, other than murder, and has been sentenced to a term of imprisonment of over six months;

(f) the person has been convicted elsewhere of an offence which would, if committed in Scotland, constitute—

   (i) murder; or

   (ii) subject to paragraph (4), a criminal offence, other than murder, and been sentenced to a term of imprisonment of over six months;

(**a**) Sections 32A and 32B were inserted by section 8 of the National Health Service (Amendment) Act 1995 (c.31). Section 32A(2) was amended by paragraph 51 of schedule 4 of the Health Act 1999 ("the 1999 Act"), and section 26(7) of the Smoking, Health and Social Care (Scotland) Act 2005 ("the 2005 Act"). Section 32B(1) was amended by the paragraph 52 of schedule 4 of 1999 Act and paragraph 1 of schedule 3 of the 2005 Act.

(g) the person has been convicted of an offence referred to in schedule 1 of the Criminal Procedure (Scotland) Act 1995(**a**)or schedule 1 of the Children and Young Persons Act 1933(**b**);

(h) the person has—

    (i) had sequestration of the person's estate awarded or been adjudged bankrupt unless (in either case) the person has been discharged or the bankruptcy order has been annulled;

    (ii) been made the subject of a bankruptcy restrictions order or an interim bankruptcy restrictions order under—

        (aa) schedule 4A of the Insolvency Act 1986(**c**);

        (bb) schedule 2A of the Insolvency (Northern Ireland) Order 1989(**d**);

        (cc) sections 56A to 56K of the Bankruptcy (Scotland) Act 1985(**e**); or

        (dd) sections 155 to 160 of the Bankruptcy (Scotland) Act 2016(**f**),

    unless that order has ceased to have effect or has been annulled; or

    (iii) made a composition or arrangement with, or granted a trust deed for, the person's creditors unless the person has been discharged in respect of it;

(i) there is—

    (i) an administrator, administrative receiver or receiver is appointed in respect of it; or

    (ii) an administration order made in respect of it under schedule B1 of the Insolvency Act 1986(**g**);

(j) that person is a partnership or limited liability partnership and—

    (i) a dissolution of the partnership or limited liability partnership has been ordered by any competent court, tribunal or arbitrator; or

    (ii) an event has happened that makes it unlawful for the business of the partnership or limited liability partnership to continue, or for members of the partnership or limited liability partnership to carry on in partnership or limited liability partnership;

(k) the person has been—

    (i) removed under section 34 of the Charities and Trustee Investment (Scotland) Act 2005 (powers of the Court of Session)(**h**), from being concerned in the management or control of any body; or

    (ii) removed from the office of charity trustee or trustee for a charity by an order made by the Charity Commission for England and Wales or the High Court on the grounds of any misconduct or mismanagement in the administration of the charity for which the person was responsible or to which the person was privy, or which the person by that person's conduct contributed to or facilitated;

(**a**) 1995 c.46. Schedule 1 was amended by section 7(1) of the Prohibition of Female Genital Mutilation (Scotland) Act 2005 (asp 8), paragraph 2 of schedule 1 of the Protection of Children and Prevention of Sexual Offences (Scotland) Act 2005 (asp 9), paragraph 2 of schedule 5 of the Sexual Offences (Scotland) Act 2009 (asp 9) and section 41 of the Criminal Justice and Licensing (Scotland) Act 2010 (asp 13).

(**b**) 1933 c.12. Schedule 1 was amended by paragraph 52 of schedule 4 of the Sexual Offences Act 1956 (c.69), paragraph 170(2) of schedule 16 of the Criminal Justice Act 1988 (c.33), paragraph 7 of schedule 6 of the Sexual Offences Act 2003 (c.42) and paragraph 1 of schedule 5 of the Modern Slavery Act 2015 (c.3).

(**c**) 1986 c.45. Schedule 4A was inserted by section 257 and paragraph 1 of schedule 20 of the Enterprise Act 2002 (c.40) ("the 2002 Act") and was amended by paragraph 63 of the Enterprise and Regulatory Reform Act 2013 (c.24).

(**d**) S.I. 1989/2405 (N.I. 19). schedule 2A was inserted by S.I. 2005/1455 (N.I. 10).

(**e**) 1985 c.66. Sections 56A to 56K were inserted by section 2(1) of the Bankruptcy and Diligence etc. (Scotland) Act 2007 (asp 3), amended by the Bankruptcy and Debt Advice (Scotland) Act 2014 (asp 11) and repealed by Part 1 of schedule 9 of the Bankruptcy (Scotland) Act 2016 (asp 21).

(**f**) 2016 asp 21.

(**g**) Schedule B1 was inserted by paragraph 1 of schedule 16 of the 2002 Act.

(**h**) 2005 asp 10. Section 34 was amended by section 122 of the Public Services Reform (Scotland) Act 2010 (asp 8).

(l) the person is subject to—

    (i) a disqualification order under section 1 of the Company Directors Disqualification Act 1986(**a**);

    (ii) a disqualification undertaking under section 1A of that Act(**b**);

    (iii) a disqualification order under article 3 of the Company Directors Disqualification (Northern Ireland) Order 2002(**c**);

    (iv) a disqualification undertaking under article 4 of that Order(**d**); or

    (v) an order under section 429(2)(b) of the Insolvency Act 1986(**e**) (failure to pay under county court administration order); or

(m) the person falls within regulation 6(2)(d) (general conditions relating to all contracts) of the National Health Service (General Medical Services Contracts) Regulations 2015(**f**).

(3) A person will not fall within paragraph (2)(b) where the Health Board is satisfied that the disqualification or suspension from practising is imposed by a licensing body outside the United Kingdom and it does not make the person unsuitable to be—

(a) a contractor;

(b) a partner, in the case of a contract with a partnership;

(c) a member, in the case of a contract with a limited liability partnership;

(d) in the case of a contract with a company—

    (i) a member of the company; or

    (ii) a director or secretary of the company,

as the case may be.

(4) A person will not fall within paragraph (2)(f)(ii) where the Health Board is satisfied that the conviction does not make the person unsuitable to be—

(a) a contractor;

(b) a partner, in the case of a contract with a partnership;

(c) a member in the case of a contract with a limited liability partnership;

(d) in the case of a contract with a company—

    (i) a member of the company; or

    (ii) a director or secretary of the company,

as the case may be.

(5) In this regulation, "health service body" does not include any person who is to be regarded as a health service body in accordance with regulation 13.

Further conditions relating to all contracts

7.—(1) For the purposes of section 17L(4) of the Act(**g**) (eligibility to be contractor under general medical services contract), a person regularly performs or is engaged in the day to day provision of primary medical services where, subject to paragraphs (2) and (3), that person so performs or is so engaged, or will so perform or so engage, for no less than a total of 10 hours in each week for the duration of the contract.

(**a**) 1986 c.46. Section 1 was amended by section 5 and paragraph 2 of schedule 4 of the Insolvency Act 2000 (c.39) ("the 2000 Act"), section 204 of the 2002 Act and paragraph 2 of schedule 7 of the Small Business, Enterprise and Employment Act 2015 (c.26) ("the 2015 Act").

(**b**) Section 1A was inserted by S.I. 2005/1454 (N.I. 9) and section 6(2) of the 2000 Act and amended by paragraph 3 of schedule 7 of the 2015 Act.

(**c**) S.I. 2002/3150 (N.I. 4). Article 3 was amended by paragraph 9 of schedule 8 of the 2015 Act.

(**d**) Article 4 was amended by paragraph 9 of schedule 8 of the 2015 Act.

(**e**) Section 429 was amended by paragraph 15 of schedule 23 of the Enterprise Act 2002.

(**f**) S.I. 2015/1862.

(**g**) Section 17L was substituted by section 39 of the Tobacco and Primary Medical Services (Scotland) Act 2010 asp 3.

(2) For the purposes of section 17L(5)(b) of the Act, references in section 17L(4) to a person who is performing or is engaged in the provision of services, include a person who has performed or been engaged in providing the services within 6 months prior to the contract being entered into.

(3) For the purposes of section 17L(6) of the Act, the prescribed circumstances in which a period of time in which a person is not performing or is not engaged in the provision of primary medical services is to be disregarded for the purposes of determining whether the person regularly performs or is engaged in the day to day provision of those services are where the period of time is—

    (a) a period of annual leave, as determined by the period of annual leave entitlement of the said person;

    (b) a local or public holiday in Scotland;

    (c) a period of—

        (i) maternity leave;

        (ii) paternity leave;

        (iii) adoption leave;

        (iv) parental leave; or

        (v) shared parental leave,

    as determined by the period of entitlement of the said person;

    (d) a period of time when a person has been incapable of work due to sickness, injury or pregnancy;

    (e) a period of time of up to a maximum of 12 months, when a person is undertaking approved study or training;

    (f) a period of service as a medical practitioner employed under a contract of service by the Ministry of Defence, whether or not as a member of the armed forces of the Crown, provided that the medical practitioner is entered on the General Practitioner Register kept by virtue of section 34C of the Medical Act 1983(a);

    (g) a period of whole time service in the armed forces of the Crown in a national emergency, as a volunteer or otherwise, or a compulsory whole time service in those forces, including any service resulting from any reserve liability, or any equivalent service by a person liable for compulsory whole-time service in those forces; or

    (h) any period during which the person has been suspended by a professional regulatory body, a Health Board or the Tribunal where that person was suspended after the contract with the Health Board was entered into.

(4) For the purposes of this regulation, "approved study or training" means study or training which is relevant for the purposes of the contractor carrying out the obligations under the contract effectively, and which has been approved by the appropriate partner, member or person responsible for training and development.

Reasons

8.—(1) Where a Health Board is of the view that the conditions in regulations 5, 6 or 7 for entering into a contract are not met, it must notify in writing the person intending to enter into the contract of the Health Board's view and its reasons for that view and of that person's right of appeal under regulation 9.

(2) The Health Board must also notify in writing of its view and its reasons for that view—

    (a) any partner in the partnership that is notified under paragraph (1);

    (b) any member of a limited liability partnership that is notified under paragraph (1);

(a) 1983 c.54. Section 34C was inserted by S.I. 2010/234.

(c) any member, or a director or secretary, of a company that is notified under paragraph (1) where its reasons for that view relates to that person or persons.

Appeal

9. A person who has been served with a notice under regulation 8(1) may appeal to the Scottish Ministers against the decision of the Health Board by giving notice in writing to the Scottish Ministers within the period of 28 days beginning on the day that the Health Board served its notice.

Continuing conditions relating to contracts

10.—(1) The following conditions apply for the duration of the contract—
  (a) in the case of a contract entered into with a medical practitioner, that practitioner must be a general medical practitioner;
  (b) in the case of a contract entered into prior to 22nd December 2010 with a partnership—
    (i) at least one partner (who must not be a limited partner) must be a general medical practitioner; and
    (ii) any other partner who is a medical practitioner must—
      (aa) be a general medical practitioner; or
      (bb) be employed, in Scotland, by a Health Board, in England and Wales, by a Local Health Board, NHS trust, NHS foundation trust or, in Northern Ireland, by a Health and Social Care trust; and
    (iii) all the other partners must be individuals;
  (c) in the case of a contract entered into on or after 22nd December 2010 with a partnership—
    (i) at least one partner (who must not be a limited partner) must be a general medical practitioner; and
    (ii) all the other members must be individuals;
  (d) in the case of a contract entered into with a limited liability partnership—
    (i) at least one partner must be a general medical practitioner; and
    (ii) all the other members must be individuals;
  (e) in the case of a contract entered into prior to 22nd December 2010 with a company limited by shares—
    (i) at least one share in the company must be legally and beneficially owned by a general medical practitioner; and
    (ii) any other share or shares in the company that are legally and beneficially owned by a medical practitioner must be so owned by—
      (aa) a general medical practitioner; or
      (bb) a medical practitioner who is employed, in Scotland, by a Health Board, in England and Wales, by a Local Health Board, NHS trust, NHS foundation trust or in Northern Ireland, by a Health and Social Care trust;
  (f) in the case of a contract entered into on or after 22nd December 2010 with a company—
    (i) at least one member of the company must be a general medical practitioner; and
    (ii) all the other members must be individuals.

(2) Regulation 5(5) applies to the meaning of "general medical practitioner" in paragraph (1)(a), (b), (c), (d), (e) and (f) as it applies to the meaning of "general medical practitioner" in regulation 5(1), (2)(a), (3)(a) and (4)(a).

Continuing conditions relating to contracts – sufficient involvement in patient care

11.—(1) The contractor must ensure that—

(a) for the duration of the contract while a person falls within paragraph (2)(a), that person has sufficient involvement in patient care; and

(b) where a person falls within paragraph (2)(b), that person has sufficient involvement in patient care from the date they fall within that paragraph for the rest of the duration of the contract or until they cease to fall within paragraph (2)(b)(i) to (iii), whichever is the earlier.

(2) A person falls within—

(a) this sub-paragraph if, in the case of a contract entered into on or after 22nd December 2010 with—

(i) a medical practitioner, they are that medical practitioner;

(ii) a partnership or limited liability partnership, they are a member of that partnership or limited liability partnership; or

(iii) a company, they are a member of that company; or

(b) this sub-paragraph if, in the case of a contract entered into prior to 22nd December 2010 with—

(i) a medical practitioner, they are that medical practitioner;

(ii) a partnership, they are a member of that partnership; or

(iii) a company, they are a person who legally and beneficially owns a share in that company; and

(iv) they fall within paragraph (3) or (4);

(v) they fall within paragraph (3) or (4).

(3) A person falls within this paragraph where on or after 1st April 2018—

(a) they become a partner of a partnership mentioned in sub-paragraph (2)(b)(ii); or

(b) they become a person who legally and beneficially owns a share in a company mentioned in sub-paragraph (2)(b)(iii).

(4) A person falls within this paragraph if they—

(a) do not fall within paragraph (3); and

(b) have had sufficient involvement in patient care for a period of 3 months starting on or after 1st April 2018 unless the Health Board has confirmed that the person only falls within this paragraph due to exceptional or temporary circumstances.

(5) Subject to paragraph (6), in this regulation, "sufficient involvement in patient care" means regularly performing, or being engaged in the day to day provision of, primary medical services in accordance with a general medical services contract, section 17C arrangements, or any other arrangement made in pursuance of section 2C(2) of the Act for no less than a total of 10 hours in each week.

(6) The periods of time described in regulation 7(3)(a) to (h) are to be disregarded for the purposes of determining whether a person has sufficient involvement in patient care for the purposes of this regulation.

(7) Where a person falls within paragraph (2) and then retires, the period of time following the date of retirement, which is the shorter of—

(a) the equivalent of the length of time that the person has had sufficient involvement in patient care for the purposes of the contractor's contract; and

(b) 2 years following the date of retirement,

is to be disregarded for the purposes of determining whether the person has sufficient involvement in patient care for the purposes of this regulation.

(8) The contactor must ensure that in the case of a contract entered into prior to 22nd December 2010—

(a) with a partnership, every member of that partnership who is not a medical practitioner and does not fall within paragraph (2)(b) complies with the conditions prescribed in section 17L(2)(a) and (c) of the Act as in force at 21st December 2010; and

(b) with a company, every person who legally and beneficially owns a share in that company who is not a medical practitioner and does not fall within paragraph (2)(b) complies with the conditions prescribed in section 17L(3)(b) of the Act as in force at 21st December 2010.

PART 3

PRE-CONTRACT DISPUTE RESOLUTION

Pre-contract disputes

12.—(1) If, in the course of negotiations intended to lead to a contract, the prospective parties to that contract are unable to agree on a particular term of the contract, either party may refer the terms of the proposed contract to the Scottish Ministers to consider and determine the matter.

(2) Disputes referred to the Scottish Ministers in accordance with paragraph (1) must be considered and determined in accordance with—

(a) the NHS dispute resolution procedure, as if—

(i) in paragraph 91(3)(b) of schedule 6, "contract" read "terms of the proposed contract";

(ii) paragraph 92(2) of schedule 6 were omitted; and

(b) paragraph (3) of this regulation.

(3) In the case of a dispute referred to the Scottish Ministers under paragraph (1), the determination of the adjudicator—

(a) may specify terms to be included in the proposed contract;

(b) may require the Health Board to proceed with the proposed contract but may not require the proposed contractor to proceed with the proposed contract; and

(c) is binding upon the prospective parties to the contract.

PART 4

HEALTH SERVICE BODY STATUS

Health service body status

13.—(1) Where a proposed contractor elects, in a written notice served on the Health Board at any time prior to the contract being entered into, to be regarded as a health service body for any purposes of section 17A of the Act(**a**) (NHS Contracts), it will be so regarded from the date on which the contract is entered into but only for the purposes of that contract.

(**a**) Section 17A was inserted by section 30 of the National Health Service and Community Care Act 1990 (c.19) ("the 1990 Act"). Section 17A was moved under a new heading entitled "NHS Contracts" by section 31 of the National Health Service (Primary Care) Act 1997 (c.46) ("the 1997 Act"). Section 17 was amended by paragraph 102 of schedule 1 of the Health Authorities Act 1995 (c.17), paragraph 36 of schedule 2 of the 1997 Act, paragraph 46 of schedule 4 and paragraph 1 of schedule 5 of the Health Act 1999 (c.8), paragraph 1 of schedule 14 of the Health and Social Care (Community Health and Standards) Act 2003 (c.43), paragraph 8 of schedule 17 of the Public Services Reform (Scotland) Act 2010 (asp 8) and paragraph 2 of schedule 21 of the Health and Social Care Act 2012 (c.7).

(2) Where a contract is made with a partnership, and that partnership is to be regarded as a health service body in accordance with paragraph (1) or (4), the contractor will, subject to paragraph (3), continue to be regarded as a health service body for any purposes of section 17A of the Act for as long as that contract continues irrespective of any change in the membership of the partnership.

(3) A contractor may at any time request in writing a variation of the contract to include or remove provision from the contract that the contract is an NHS contract and, if the contractor does so—

  (a) the Health Board must agree to the variation; and

  (b) the procedure in paragraph 94(1) of schedule 6 applies.

(4) If, pursuant to paragraph (3), the Health Board agrees to the variation to the contract, the contractor will—

  (a) be regarded; or

  (b) subject to paragraph (6), cease to be regarded,

as a health service body for any purposes of section 17A of the Act from the date that variation is to take effect pursuant to paragraph 94(1) of schedule 6.

(5) Subject to paragraph (6), a contractor ceases to be a health service body for the purposes of section 17A of the Act if the contract terminates.

(6) Where a contractor ceases to be a health service body pursuant to—

  (a) paragraph (4), the contractor will, if the contractor or the Health Board has referred any matter to the Scottish Ministers for determination under section 17A(4) of the Act before the contractor ceases to be a health service body, be bound by the determination of the adjudicator;

  (b) paragraph (5), it will continue to be regarded as a health service body for the purposes of the NHS dispute resolution procedure where that procedure has been commenced—

    (i) before the termination of the contract; or

    (ii) after the termination of the contract, whether in connection with or arising out of the termination of the contract or otherwise,

for which purposes it ceases to be such a body on the conclusion of that procedure.

(7) If, pursuant to paragraph (1) or (4), a contractor is to be regarded as a health service body, section 17A has effect in relation to such a person subject to the following modifications:—

  (a) for subsection (4), substitute—

    "(4) Whether or not an arrangement which constitutes an NHS contract would, apart from this subsection, be a contract in law, it shall not be regarded for any purpose as giving rise to contractual rights or liabilities but, if any dispute arises out of or in connection with the NHS contract, either party may refer the matter to the Scottish Ministers for determination in accordance with the NHS dispute resolution procedure specified in paragraphs 91 and 92 of schedule 6 of the National Health Service (General Medical Services Contracts) (Scotland) Regulations 2018.";

  (b) after subsection (4), insert—

    "(4A) In subsection (4), the reference to "any dispute arises out of or in connection with the NHS contract" includes any dispute arising out of or in connection with the termination of the contract.";

  (c) subsections (5), (6) and (7) do not apply; and

  (d) in subsections (8) and (9), for any reference to "the person appointed under subsection (6)", substitute a reference to "the panel appointed by the Scottish Ministers under paragraph 91 of schedule 6 of the National Health Service (General Medical Services Contracts) (Scotland) Regulations 2018".

PART 5

CONTRACTS: MANDATORY TERMS

Parties to the contract

14. A contract must specify—

(a) the names of the parties;

(b) in the case of a partnership—

(i) whether or not it is a limited partnership; and

(ii) the names of the partners and, in the case of a limited partnership, their status as a general or limited partner; and

(c) in the case of each party, the address to which official correspondence and notices should be sent.

NHS contracts

15. If the contractor is to be regarded as a health service body pursuant to regulation 13, the contract must state that it is an NHS contract.

Contracts with a partnership

16.—(1) Where the contract is with a partnership, the contract is to be treated as made with the partnership as it is from time to time constituted, and the contract must make specific provision to this effect.

(2) Where the contract is with a partnership, the contractor must be required by the terms of the contract to ensure that any person who becomes a member of the partnership after the contract has come into force is bound automatically by the contract whether by virtue of a partnership deed or otherwise.

(3) For the avoidance of doubt, in this regulation, a reference to a "partnership" does not include a reference to a limited liability partnership.

Duration

17.—(1) Except in the circumstances specified in paragraph (2), a contract must provide for it to subsist until it is terminated in accordance with the terms of the contract or the general law.

(2) The circumstances referred to in paragraph (1) are that the Health Board wishes to enter into a temporary contract for a period not exceeding twelve months for the provision of services to the former patients of a contractor, following the termination of that contractor's contract.

(3) Either party to a prospective contract to which paragraph (2) applies may, if they wish to do so, invite the area medical committee for the area of the Health Board to participate in the negotiations intended to lead to such a contract.

Essential services

18.—(1) For the purposes of section 17K(1) of the Act (mandatory contract terms: provision of prescribed primary medical services)(**a**), the services which must be provided under a general medical services contract ("essential services") are the services described in paragraphs (3), (5), (6) and (8).

(2) Subject to regulation 23, a contractor must provide the services described in paragraphs (3) and (5) throughout core hours.

(**a**) Section 17K was inserted by section 4 of the Primary Medical Services (Scotland) Act 2004 (asp 1).

(3) The services described in this paragraph are services required for the management of its registered patients and temporary residents who are, or believe themselves to be—

    (a) ill, with conditions from which recovery is generally expected;

    (b) terminally ill; or

    (c) suffering from chronic disease,

delivered in the manner determined by the practice in discussion with the patient.

(4) For the purposes of paragraph (3)—

    (a) "disease" means a disease included in the list of three-character categories contained in the tenth revision of the International Statistical Classification of Diseases and Related Health Problems(**a**); and

    (b) "management" includes—

        (i) offering consultation and, where appropriate, physical examination for the purpose of identifying the need, if any, for treatment or further investigation; and

        (ii) the making available of such treatment or further investigation as is necessary and appropriate, including the referral of the patient for other services under the Act and liaison with other health care professionals involved in the patient's treatment and care.

(5) The services described in this paragraph are the provision of appropriate ongoing treatment and care to all registered patients and temporary residents taking account of their specific needs including—

    (a) the provision of advice in connection with the patient's health, including relevant health promotion advice; and

    (b) the referral of the patient for other services under the Act.

(6) A contractor must provide primary medical services required in core hours, taking into account the contractor's safety and the availability of other options for care, for the immediately necessary treatment of any person to whom the contractor has been requested to provide treatment owing to an accident or emergency at any place in its practice area.

(7) In paragraph (6), "emergency" includes any medical emergency whether or not related to services provided under the contract.

(8) A contractor must provide primary medical services required in core hours for the immediately necessary treatment of any person falling within paragraph (9) who requests such treatment, for the period specified in paragraph (10).

(9) A person falls within this paragraph if they are a person—

    (a) whose application for inclusion in the contractor's list of patients has been refused in accordance with paragraph 14 of schedule 6 and who is not registered with another provider of essential services (or their equivalent) in the area of the Health Board;

    (b) whose application for acceptance as a temporary resident has been refused in accordance with paragraph 14 of schedule 6; or

    (c) who is present in the contractor's practice area for less than 24 hours.

(10) The period referred to in paragraph (8) is—

    (a) in the case of paragraph (9)(a) 14 days beginning with the date on which that person's application was refused or until that person has been subsequently registered elsewhere for the provision of essential services (or their equivalent), whichever occurs first;

    (b) in the case of paragraph (9)(b), 14 days beginning with the date on which that person's application was rejected or until that person has been subsequently accepted elsewhere as a temporary resident, whichever occurs first; and

---

(**a**) World Health Organisation, 2010 ISBN 9789241548342.

(c) in the case of paragraph (9)(c), 24 hours or such shorter period as the person is present in the contractor's practice area.

Additional services

19. A contract which includes the provision of any additional services must—

(a) in relation to all such services, contain a term which has the same effect as that specified in paragraph 1 of schedule 1; and

(b) in relation to each such service, contain terms which have the same effect as those specified in schedule 1, which are relevant to that service.

Opt outs of additional services

20. Where a contract provides for the contractor to provide an additional service that is to be funded under the global sum, the contract must contain terms relating to the procedure for opting out of additional services which have the same effect as those specified in schedule 2, except paragraph 3(14) to (16) of that schedule.

Services generally

21.—(1) A contract must specify—

(a) the services to be provided;

(b) subject to paragraph (2), the address of each of the premises to be used by the contractor or any sub-contractor for the provision of such services;

(c) to whom such services are to be provided;

(d) the area as respects which persons resident in it will, subject to any other terms of the contract relating to patient registration, be entitled to—

   (i) register with the contractor; or

   (ii) seek acceptance by the contractor as a temporary resident; and

(e) whether, at the date on which the contract comes into force, the contractor's list of patients is open or closed.

(2) The premises referred to in paragraph (1)(b) do not include—

(a) the homes of patients; or

(b) any other premises where services are provided on an emergency basis.

(3) Where, on the date on which the contract is signed, the Health Board is not satisfied that all or any of the premises specified in accordance with paragraph (1)(b) meet the requirements set out in paragraph 1 of schedule 6, the contract must include a plan, drawn up jointly by the Health Board and the contractor, which specifies—

(a) the steps to be taken by the contractor to bring the premises up to the relevant standard;

(b) any financial support that may be available from the Health Board; and

(c) the timescale on which the steps referred to in sub-paragraph (a) will be taken.

(4) Where, in accordance with paragraph (1)(e), the contract specifies that the contractor's list of patients is closed, it must also specify in relation to that closure each of the items listed in paragraph 26(9)(a) to (d) of schedule 6.

Services generally

22.—(1) Except in the case of the services referred to in paragraph (2), the contract must state the period (if any) for which the services are to be provided.

(2) The services referred to in paragraph (1) are—

(a) essential services; and

(b) additional services funded under the global sum.

Services generally

23. A contract must contain a term which requires the contractor in core hours—
   (a) to provide—
      (i) essential services; and
      (ii) additional services funded under the global sum,

      at such times, within core hours, as are appropriate to meet the reasonable needs of the contractor's patients; and
   (b) to have in place arrangements for the contractor's patients to access such services throughout the core hours in case of emergency.

Additional obligations in relation to practice premises

24.—(1) A contractor who receives financial assistance must comply with the obligations set out in schedule 3 throughout the period that the contractor receives that assistance and a term to this effect must be included in the contract.

(2) In this regulation, "financial assistance" means financial assistance from a Health Board or the Scottish Ministers in the form of—
   (a) a recurring payment to the contractor of—
      (i) the contractor's owner-occupier borrowing costs;
      (ii) notional rent payments to the contractor as an owner-occupier; or
      (iii) reimbursement of the contractor's rent payments,

      in accordance with directions under sections 2(5) and 17M(3) of the Act(**a**); or
   (b) a loan secured over the practice premises.

Certificates

25.—(1) A contract must contain a term which has the effect of requiring the contractor to issue free of charge to a patient or a patient's personal representatives any medical certificate of a description prescribed in column 1 of schedule 4, which is reasonably required under or for the purposes of the enactments specified in relation to the certificate in column 2 of that schedule, except where, for the condition to which the certificate relates, the patient—
   (a) is being attended by a medical practitioner or an alternative provider for the relevant certificate who is not—
      (i) employed or engaged by the contractor;
      (ii) in the case of a contract with a partnership, one of the partners;
      (iii) in the case of a contract with a limited liability partnership, one of the members; or
      (iv) in the case of a contract with a company, one of the members; or
   (b) is not being treated by or under the supervision of a health care professional.

(2) The exception in paragraph (1)(a) will not apply where the certificate is a doctor's statement issued in accordance with regulation 2(1) of the Social Security (Medical Evidence) Regulations 1976(**b**) (evidence of incapacity for work, limited capability for work and confinement) or regulation 2(1) of the Statutory Sick Pay (Medical Evidence) Regulations 1985(**c**) (medical information).

(**a**)   Section 17M was inserted by section 4 of the Primary Medical Services (Scotland) Act 2004.
(**b**)   S.I. 1976/615. Regulation 2(1) was substituted by S.I. 2010/137.
(**c**)   S.I. 1985/1604. Regulation 2(1) was substituted by S.I. 2010/137.

(3) The contract must contain a term which has the effect of providing that the contractor's obligation to issue any medical certificate prescribed in column 1 of schedule 4 can be discharged on behalf of the contractor by an alternative provider for the relevant medical certificate.

(4) In this regulation "alternative provider" means another health care professional(a) who falls within the description of alternative providers specified in column 3 of schedule 4 in relation to the relevant medical certificate prescribed in column 1 of that schedule.

Finance

26.—(1) Subject to paragraph (2), the contract must contain a term which has the effect of requiring the Health Board to make payments to the contractor under the contract promptly and in accordance with both the terms of the contract and any other conditions relating to the payment contained in directions given by the Scottish Ministers under section 17M of the Act.

(2) The obligation referred to in paragraph (1) is subject to any right the Health Board may have to set off, against any amount payable to the contractor under the contract, any amount—

(a) that is owed by the contractor to the Health Board under the contract; or

(b) that the Health Board may withhold from the contractor in accordance with the terms of the contract or any other applicable provisions contained in directions given by the Scottish Ministers under section 17M of the Act.

Finance

27. The contract must contain a term to the effect that where, pursuant to any directions of the Scottish Ministers under sections 2(5) and 17M(3) of the Act, a Health Board is required to make a payment to a contractor under a contract but subject to conditions, those conditions are to be a term of the contract.

Fees and charges

28.—(1) The contract must contain terms relating to fees and charges which have the same effect as those set out in paragraphs (2) to (4).

(2) The contractor must not, either itself or through any other person, demand or accept from any of its patients a fee or other remuneration, for the benefit of the contractor or another person, for—

(a) the provision of any treatment whether under the contract or otherwise; or

(b) any prescription for any drug, medicine or appliance,

except in the circumstances set out in schedule 5.

(3) Where a person applies to a contractor for the provision of essential services and claims to be on that contractor's list of patients, but the contractor has reasonable doubts about that person's claim, the contractor must give any necessary treatment and will be entitled to demand and accept a reasonable fee in accordance with paragraph (1)(e) of schedule 5, subject to the provision for repayment contained in paragraph (4).

(4) Where a person from whom a contractor received a fee under paragraph (e) of schedule 5 applies to the Health Board for a refund within 14 days of payment of the fee (or such longer period not exceeding one month as the Health Board may allow, if it is satisfied that the failure to apply within 14 days was reasonable) and the Health Board is satisfied that the person was on the contractor's list of patients when the treatment was given, the Health Board may recover the amount of the fee from the contractor, by deduction from the contractor's remuneration or otherwise, and must pay that amount to the person who paid the fee.

(a) "Health care professional" includes nurses and midwives registered with the Nursing and Midwifery Council.

Arrangements on termination

29. A contract must make suitable provision for arrangements on termination of the contract, including the consequences (whether financial or otherwise) of the contract ending.

Other contractual terms

30.—(1) A contract must, unless it is of a type or nature to which a particular provision does not apply, contain other terms which have the same effect as those specified in schedule 6, except paragraphs 28(5) to (7), 32(5) to (9), 33(3), 91(5) to (15) and 92.

(2) The paragraphs specified in paragraph (1) have effect in relation to the matters set out in those paragraphs.

Implied contract terms

31.—(1) Where a contract fails to include any required term, such a term is to be an implied term of the contract.

(2) A contract must contain a term which has the effect that—

    (a) where, or to the extent that a term is a required term and such a required term is omitted, either in whole or in part, from the express terms of the contract; and

    (b) as a result, the contract does not expressly include that required term in full,

that required term, to the extent that it was omitted from the express terms of the contract, is to be an implied term of the contract.

(3) In the event of, and only to the extent of, any conflict between any term that must be implied in accordance with this regulation, the clauses of the contract and the schedules of the contract, the following order of precedence applies—

    (a) any required term that is implied in accordance with this regulation;

    (b) the clauses of the contract; and

    (c) the schedules of the contract.

(4) A "required term" is any term which is required to be included in the contract by virtue of these Regulations, including any term which is required by an amendment, extension, re-enactment, or consolidation of these Regulations, whether before or after the commencement of the contract.

PART 6

FUNCTIONS OF AREA MEDICAL COMMITTEE

Functions of area medical committee

32.—(1) The functions of an area medical committee which are prescribed for the purposes of section 9(6) of the Act (local consultative committees) are—

    (a) the functions which are conferred upon it by these Regulations or by any order made under section 7 of the 2004 Act;

    (b) the making of arrangements for the medical examination of a medical practitioner specified in paragraph (2), where the contractor or the Health Board is concerned that the medical practitioner is incapable of adequately providing services under the contract and the contractor or the Health Board so requests with the agreement of the medical practitioner concerned;

    (c) the consideration of the report of any medical examination arranged in accordance with sub-paragraph (b) and the making of a written report as to the capability of the medical practitioner of adequately providing services under the contract to the medical practitioner concerned, the contractor and the Health Board with whom the contractor holds a contract;

(d) the making of all necessary arrangements and performance of all functions reasonably required to set up, support and facilitate any improvement or quality arrangement of a cluster or any other person as required in any directions given by Scottish Ministers under section 2(5) of the Act(**a**); and

(e) the making of all necessary arrangements and performance of all necessary functions reasonably required to support and facilitate local dispute resolution processes in its area, including any local dispute resolution process relating to remuneration and conditions of service.

(2) The medical practitioner referred to in paragraph (1)(b) is a medical practitioner who is—

(a) a contractor;

(b) where the contractor is a partnership, any partner in the partnership; or

(c) where the contractor is a limited liability partnership, any member of the limited liability partnership; or

(d) where the contractor is a company, any member of that company.

PART 7

TRANSITIONAL PROVISIONS

Out of hours

33.—(1) Where on 31st March 2018 a contract included a requirement to provide out of hours services pursuant to regulation 32 of the 2004 Regulations—

(a) the contract must continue to require the contractor to provide out of hours services; and

(b) despite the revocation of the 2004 Regulations(**b**), the provisions of the 2004 Regulations referred to in paragraph (2) will continue to have effect in relation to that contract on and after 1st April 2018 as they had effect immediately before that date,

until one of the end dates in paragraph (3) occurs.

(2) The provisions of the 2004 Regulations are—

(a) regulation 2, only in so far as that regulation relates to the definitions for "out of hours period" and "out of hours services";

(b) regulations 30, 31 and 32;

(c) paragraphs 10, 11(**c**), 12(c), 13(c), 63, 64 and 65 of schedule 5;

(d) schedule 6; and

(e) paragraph 18 of schedule 8.

(3) The end dates referred to in paragraph (1) are—

(a) where a contractor—

(i) has served an out of hours opt out notice under paragraph 4(2) of schedule 2 of the 2004 Regulations in the period from 12th November 2017 to 31st March 2018; or

(ii) serves on the Health Board a written notice stating that the contractor wishes to terminate its obligation to provide out of hours services under its contract,

---

(**a**) Section 2(5) was amended by paragraph 19(1) of schedule 9 of the National Health Service and Community Care Act 1990 (c.19).
(**b**) S.S.I. 2004/115 is revoked by regulation 34 and schedule 9 of these Regulations.
(**c**) Paragraph 11 of schedule 5 of S.S.I. 2004/115 was amended by S.S.I. 2011/211.

the end date is the date 9 months after the date of service of the notice or such earlier date as the Health Board and the contactor agree; and

(b) where on or after 1st April 2018, the contractor enters into an arrangement with the Health Board to provide out of hours services, the end date is the date the contractor commences providing out of hours services under the arrangement, or such other date as the Health Board and the contractor agree.

(4) The contractor's duty to provide out of hours services under the contract will terminate with effect from 0800 hours on the end date referred to in paragraph (3) unless the Health Board and the contractor agree a different date or time.

(5) Nothing in paragraphs (1) to (4) prevents the contractor and the Health Board from agreeing a different date for the termination of the contractor's duty under the contract to provide out of hours services and accordingly varying the contract in accordance with paragraph 94(1) of schedule 6.

(6) Prior to the contactor's duty to provide out of hours services under the contract ceasing, the Health Board and the contactor must discuss how to inform patients of any change to the out of hours services which the contractor provides.

(7) The contractor must, if requested by the Health Board, inform the contractor's registered patients of the change in service by the contractor and the arrangements made for them to receive out of hours services by—

(a) placing a notice in the practice's waiting room; and

(b) including the information in the practice leaflet.

PART 8

SUPPLEMENTARY

Revocations

34. The enactments specified in column 1 of schedule 9 are hereby revoked to the extent specified in column 3 of that schedule.

Consequential amendments

35. Schedule 10 (consequential amendments) has effect.

AILEEN CAMPBELL
Authorised to sign by the Scottish Ministers

St Andrew's House,
Edinburgh
15th February 2018

SCHEDULE 1

Regulation 19

ADDITIONAL SERVICES

Additional services generally

1. The contractor must provide, in relation to each additional service, such facilities and equipment as are necessary to enable it properly to perform that service.

Cervical screening

2.—(1) A contractor whose contract includes the provision of cervical screening services must—

- (a) provide all the services described in sub-paragraph (2); and
- (b) make such records as are referred to in sub-paragraph (3).

(2) The services referred to in sub-paragraph (1)(a) are—

- (a) the provision of any necessary information and advice to assist women identified by the Health Board as recommended nationally for a cervical screening test in making an informed decision as to participation in the NHS Scotland Cervical Screening Programme;
- (b) the performance of cervical screening tests on women who have agreed to participate in that Programme;
- (c) arranging for women to be informed of the results of the test; and
- (d) ensuring that test results are followed up appropriately.

(3) The records referred to in sub-paragraph (1)(b) are an accurate record of the carrying out of a cervical screening test, the result of the test and any clinical follow up requirements.

Contraceptive services

3.—(1) A contractor whose contract includes the provision of contraceptive services must make available to all its patients who request such services the services described in sub-paragraph (2).

(2) The services referred to in sub-paragraph (1) are—

- (a) the giving of advice about the full range of contraceptive methods;
- (b) where appropriate, the medical examination of patients seeking such advice;
- (c) the treatment of such patients for contraceptive purposes and the prescription of contraceptive substances and appliances (excluding the fitting and implanting of intrauterine devices and implants);
- (d) the giving of advice about emergency contraception and, where appropriate, the supplying or prescribing of emergency hormonal contraception or, where the contractor has a conscientious objection to emergency contraception, a prompt referral to another provider of primary medical services who does not have such conscientious objections;
- (e) the provision of advice and referral in cases of unplanned or unwanted pregnancy, including advice about the availability of free pregnancy testing in the practice area and, where appropriate, where the contractor has a conscientious objection to the termination of pregnancy, a prompt referral to another provider of primary medical services who does not have such conscientious objections;
- (f) the giving of initial advice about sexual health promotion and sexually transmitted infections; and
- (g) the referral as necessary for specialist sexual health services, including tests for sexually transmitted infections.

Vaccinations and immunisations

4.—(1) A contractor whose contract includes the provision of vaccinations and immunisations must comply with the requirements in sub-paragraphs (2) and (3).

(2) The contractor must—

(a) offer to provide to patients all vaccinations and immunisations (excluding childhood vaccinations and immunisations) of a type and in the circumstances for which a fee is provided for in directions given under section 17M(**a**) of the Act other than influenza and pneumococcal vaccinations;

(b) provide appropriate information and advice to patients about such vaccinations and immunisations;

(c) record in the patient's record kept in accordance with paragraph 68 of schedule 6 any refusal of the offer referred to in sub-paragraph (2)(a);

(d) where the offer is accepted, administer the vaccinations and immunisations and include in the patient's record kept in accordance with paragraph 68 of schedule 6—

(i) the patient's consent to the vaccination or immunisation, or the name of the person who gave consent to the vaccination or immunisation and that person's relationship to the patient;

(ii) the batch numbers, expiry date and title of the vaccine;

(iii) the date of administration;

(iv) in a case where two vaccines are administered in close succession, the route of administration and the injection site of each vaccine;

(v) any contraindications to the vaccination or immunisation; and

(vi) any adverse reactions to the vaccination or immunisation.

(3) The contractor must ensure that all staff involved in administering vaccines are trained in the recognition and initial treatment of anaphylaxis.

Childhood vaccinations and immunisations

5.—(1) A contractor whose contract includes the provision of childhood vaccinations and immunisations must comply with the requirements in sub-paragraphs (2) and (3).

(2) The contractor must—

(a) offer to provide to children all vaccinations and immunisations of a type and in the circumstances for which a fee is provided for in directions given under section 17M of the Act;

(b) provide appropriate information and advice to patients and, where appropriate, their parents, about such vaccinations and immunisations;

(c) record in the patient's record kept in accordance with paragraph 68 of schedule 6 any refusal of the offer referred to in paragraph (a);

(d) where the offer is accepted, administer the vaccinations and immunisations and include in the patient's record kept in accordance with paragraph 68 of schedule 6—

(i) the patient's consent to the vaccination or immunisation, or the name of the person who gave consent to the vaccination or immunisation and that person's relationship to the patient;

(ii) the batch numbers, expiry date and title of the vaccine;

(iii) the date of administration;

(iv) in a case where two vaccines are administered in close succession, the route of administration and the injection site of each vaccine;

(**a**) Section 17M was inserted into the Act by section 4 of the Primary Medical Services (Scotland) Act 2004 (asp 1).

(v) any contraindications to the vaccination or immunisation; and

(vi) any adverse reactions to the vaccination or immunisation.

(3) The contractor must ensure that all staff involved in administering vaccines are trained in the recognition and initial treatment of anaphylaxis.

Child health surveillance

6.—(1) A contractor whose contract includes the provision of child health surveillance services must, in respect of any child under the age of 5 for whom it has responsibility under the contract—

(a) provide all the services described in sub-paragraph (2), other than any examination so described which the parent refuses to allow the child to undergo, until the date upon which the child attains the age of 5 years; and

(b) maintain such records as are specified in sub-paragraph (3).

(2) The services referred to in sub-paragraph (1)(a) are—

(a) the monitoring—

(i) by the consideration of any information concerning the child received by or on behalf of the contractor; and

(ii) on any occasion when the child is examined or observed by or on behalf of the contractor (whether pursuant to sub-paragraph 2(b), or otherwise),

of the health, well-being and physical, mental and social development (all of which characteristics are referred to in this paragraph as "development") of the child while under the age of 5 years with a view to detecting any deviations from normal development; and

(b) the examination of the child at a frequency that has been agreed with the Health Board in accordance with the nationally agreed evidence based programme set out in the fourth edition of "Health for all Children"(**a**).

(3) The records mentioned in sub-paragraph (1)(b) are an accurate record of—

(a) the development of the child while under the age of 5 years, compiled as soon as is reasonably practicable following the first examination of that child and, where appropriate, amended following each subsequent examination mentioned in that sub-paragraph; and

(b) the responses (if any) to offers made to the child's parent for the child to undergo any examination referred to in sub-paragraph (2)(b).

Maternity medical services

7.—(1) A contractor whose contract includes the provision of maternity medical services must provide—

(a) to female patients who have been diagnosed as pregnant all necessary maternity medical services throughout the ante-natal period;

(b) to female patients and their babies all necessary maternity medical services throughout the post-natal period other than neonatal checks;

(c) all necessary maternity medical services to female patients whose pregnancy has terminated as a result of miscarriage or abortion or, where the contractor has a conscientious objection to the termination of pregnancy, prompt referral to another provider of primary medical services who does not have such conscientious objections.

(2) In this paragraph—

"ante-natal period" means the period from the start of the pregnancy to the onset of labour;

(**a**) David Hall and David Elliman, January 2003, Oxford University Press, ISBN 10: 01985188X, ISBN 13: 97801 98515883.

"maternity medical services" means—

(a) in relation to female patients (other than babies) all primary medical services relating to pregnancy, excluding intra partum care; and

(b) in relation to babies, any primary medical services necessary in their first 14 days of life; and

"post-natal period" means the period starting from the conclusion of delivery of the baby or the patient's discharge from secondary care services, whichever is the later, and ending on the fourteenth day after the birth.

SCHEDULE 2

Regulation 20

OPT OUTS OF ADDITIONAL SERVICES

Opt outs of additional services: general

1.—(1) In this schedule—

"opt out notice" means a notice given under sub-paragraph (5) to opt out permanently or temporarily of the provision of the additional service;

"permanent opt out" in relation to the provision of an additional service that is funded under the global sum, means the termination of the obligation under the contract for the contractor to provide that service; and "opt out permanently" is to be construed accordingly;

"permanent opt out notice" means an opt out notice to opt out permanently;

"preliminary opt out notice" means a notice given under sub-paragraph (2) that a contractor wishes to opt out permanently or temporarily of the provision of an additional service;

"temporary opt out" in relation to the provision of an additional service that is funded through the global sum, means the suspension of the obligation under the contract for the contractor to provide that service for a period of more than six months and less than twelve months and includes an extension of a temporary opt out and "opt out temporarily" and "opted out temporarily" is to be construed accordingly; and

"temporary opt out notice" means an opt out notice to opt out temporarily.

(2) A contractor who wishes to opt out permanently or temporarily must give to the Health Board in writing a preliminary opt out notice which must state the reasons for wishing to opt out.

(3) As soon as is reasonably practicable and in any event within the period of 7 days beginning on the date on which the preliminary opt out notice was received by the Health Board, the Health Board must enter into discussions with the contractor concerning the support which the Health Board may give the contractor, or concerning other changes which the Health Board or the contractor may make, which would enable the contractor to continue to provide the additional service and the Health Board and the contractor must use reasonable endeavours to achieve this aim.

(4) The discussions mentioned in sub-paragraph (3) must be completed within the period of 10 days beginning with the date on which the preliminary opt out notice was received by the Health Board or as soon as reasonably practicable thereafter.

(5) If following the discussions mentioned in sub-paragraph (3), the contractor still wishes to opt out of the provision of the additional service, it must send an opt out notice to the Health Board.

(6) An opt out notice must specify—

   (a) the additional service concerned;

   (b) whether the contractor wishes to—

      (i) opt out permanently; or

      (ii) opt out temporarily;

   (c) the reasons for wishing to opt out;

   (d) the date from which the contractor would like the opt out to commence, which must—

      (i) in the case of a temporary opt out be at least 14 days after the date of service of the opt out notice; and

      (ii) in the case of a permanent opt out must be the day either three or six months after the date of service of the opt out notice; and

   (e) in the case of a temporary opt out, the desired duration of the opt out.

(7) Where a contractor has given two previous temporary opt out notices within the period of 3 years ending with the date of the service of the latest opt out notice (whether or not the same additional service is concerned), the latest opt out notice will be treated as a permanent opt out notice (even if the opt out notice says that the contractor wishes to opt out temporarily).

(8) Paragraph 2 applies following the giving of a temporary opt out notice and paragraph 3 applies following the giving of a permanent opt out notice, or a temporary opt out notice which is treated as a permanent opt out notice pursuant to sub-paragraph (7).

Temporary opt outs and permanent opt outs following temporary opt outs

2.—(1) As soon as is reasonably practicable and in any event within the period of 7 days beginning on the date on which a temporary opt out notice mentioned in paragraph 1(5) is received, the Health Board must—

(a) approve the opt out notice and specify in accordance with sub-paragraphs (3) and (4) the date on which the temporary opt out is to commence and the date that it is to come to an end ("the end date"); or

(b) reject the opt out notice in accordance with sub-paragraph (2),

and must notify the contractor of its decision as soon as possible, including reasons for its decision.

(2) A Health Board may reject the temporary opt out notice on the ground that the contractor—

(a) is providing additional services to patients other than its own registered patients or enhanced services; or

(b) has no reasonable need temporarily to opt out having regard to its ability to deliver the additional service.

(3) The date specified by the Health Board for the commencement of the temporary opt out is to be, wherever reasonably practicable, the date requested by the contractor in its opt out notice.

(4) Before determining the end date, the Health Board must make reasonable efforts to reach agreement with the contractor.

(5) Where the Health Board approves an opt out notice, the contractor's obligation to provide the additional service specified in the notice will be suspended from the date specified by the Health Board in its decision under sub-paragraph (1), and is to remain suspended until the end date unless—

(a) the contractor and the Health Board agree in writing an earlier date, in which case the suspension is to come to an end on that date;

(b) the Health Board specifies a later date under sub-paragraph (6), in which case the suspension is to end on that date;

(c) sub-paragraph (7) applies and the contractor refers the matter to the NHS dispute resolution procedure (or, where applicable in the case of a non-NHS contract, commences court proceedings), in which case the suspension will end—

(i) where the outcome of the dispute is to uphold the decision of the Health Board, on the day after the date of the decision of the adjudicator or, as the case may be, the court;

(ii) where the outcome of the dispute is to overturn the decision of the Health Board, 28 days after the decision of the adjudicator or, as the case may be, the court; or

(iii) where the contractor ceases to pursue the NHS dispute resolution procedure or, as the case may be, court proceedings, on the day after the date that the contractor withdraws its claim or the procedure is or proceedings are otherwise terminated by the adjudicator or the court;

(d) sub-paragraph (9) applies and—
- (i) the Health Board refuses the contractor's request for a permanent opt out within the period of 28 days ending with the end date, in which case the suspension will come to an end 28 days after the end date;
- (ii) the Health Board refuses the contractor's request for a permanent opt out after the end date, in which case the suspension will come to an end 28 days after the date of service of the notice; or
- (iii) the Health Board notifies the contractor after the end date that the assessment panel has not approved its proposed decision to refuse the contractor's request to opt out permanently under sub-paragraph (16), in which case the suspension will come to an end 28 days after the date of service of the notice under that paragraph.

(6) Before the end date, a Health Board may, in exceptional circumstances and with the agreement of the contractor, notify the contractor in writing of a later date on which the temporary opt out is to come to an end, being a date no more than six months later than the end date.

(7) Where the Health Board considers that—
- (a) the contractor will be unable to satisfactorily provide the additional service at the end of the temporary opt out; and
- (b) it would not be appropriate to exercise its discretion under sub-paragraph (6) to specify a later date on which the temporary opt out is to come to an end or the contractor does not agree to a later date,

the Health Board may notify the contractor in writing at least 28 days before the end date that a permanent opt out will follow the temporary opt out.

(8) Where a Health Board notifies the contractor under sub-paragraph (7) that a permanent opt out will follow a temporary opt out, the permanent opt out must take effect immediately after the end of the temporary opt out.

(9) A contractor who has temporarily opted out may, at least three months prior to the end date, notify the Health Board in writing that it wishes to opt out permanently of the additional service in question.

(10) Where the contractor has notified the Health Board under sub-paragraph (9) that it wishes to opt out permanently, the temporary opt out must be followed by a permanent opt out beginning on the day after the end date unless the Health Board refuses the contractor's request to opt out permanently by giving notice in writing to the contractor to this effect.

(11) A Health Board may only give a notice under sub-paragraph (10) with the approval of the assessment panel.

(12) The Health Board must ensure that an assessment panel is appointed by another Health Board as soon as is practicable to consider and determine whether or not to approve the Health Board's proposed decision to refuse a permanent opt out.

(13) The Health Board must provide the assessment panel with such information as the assessment panel may reasonably require to enable it to reach a determination.

(14) Where a Health Board seeks the approval of the assessment panel to a proposed decision to refuse a permanent opt out, it must notify the contractor of having done so.

(15) If the assessment panel has not reached a decision as to whether or not to approve the Health Board's proposed decision to refuse a permanent opt out before the end date, the contractor's obligation to provide the additional service is to remain suspended until the date specified in sub-paragraph (5)(d)(ii) or (iii) (whichever is applicable).

(16) Where after the end date the assessment panel notifies the Health Board that it does not approve the Health Board's proposed decision to refuse a permanent opt out, the Health Board must notify the contractor in writing of this fact as soon as is reasonably practicable.

(17) A temporary opt out or a permanent opt out commences, and a temporary opt out ends, at 0800 hours on the relevant day unless—

(a) the day is not a working day, in which case the opt out will take effect on the next working day at 0800 hours; or

(b) the Health Board and the contractor agree a different day or time.

(18) Any decision or determination by the assessment panel for the purposes of this paragraph may be reached by a majority.

Permanent opt outs

3.—(1) In this paragraph—

"A day" is the day specified by the contractor in its permanent opt out notice to a Health Board for the commencement of the permanent opt out;

"B day" is the day six months after the date of service of the permanent opt out notice; and

"C day" is the day nine months after the date of service of the permanent opt out notice.

(2) As soon as is reasonably practicable, and in any event within the period of 28 days beginning with the date on which a permanent opt out notice under paragraph 1(5) (or temporary opt out notice which is treated as a permanent opt out notice under paragraph 1(7)) is received, the Health Board must—

(a) approve the opt out notice; or

(b) reject the opt out notice in accordance with sub-paragraph (3),

and must notify the contractor of its decision as soon as possible, including reasons for its decision, where its decision is to reject the opt out notice.

(3) A Health Board may reject the opt out notice on the ground that the contractor is providing an additional service to patients other than its registered patients or enhanced services.

(4) A contractor may not withdraw an opt out notice once it has been approved by the Health Board in accordance with sub-paragraph (2)(a) without the Health Board's agreement.

(5) If the Health Board approves the opt out notice under sub-paragraph (2)(a), it must use its reasonable endeavours to make arrangements for the contractor's registered patients to receive the additional service from an alternative provider from A day.

(6) The contractor's duty to provide the additional service will terminate on A day unless the Health Board serves a notice under sub-paragraph (7) (extending A day to B day or C day).

(7) If the Health Board is not successful in finding an alternative provider to take on the provision of the additional service from A day, then it must notify the contractor in writing of this fact not later than one month before A day, and—

(a) in a case where A day is three months after service of the opt out notice, the contractor is to continue to provide the additional service until B day unless at least one month before B day the contractor receives a notice in writing from the Health Board under sub-paragraph (8) that despite using its reasonable endeavours, it has failed to find an alternative provider to take on the provision of the additional service from B day; or

(b) in a case where A day is six months after the service of the opt out notice, the contractor is to continue to provide the additional service until C day unless at least one month before C day it receives a notice from the Health Board under sub-paragraph (11) that it has made an application to an assessment panel under sub-paragraph (10) seeking approval of the assessment panel to a decision to refuse a permanent opt out or to delay the commencement of a permanent opt out until after C day.

(8) Where in accordance with sub-paragraph (7)(a) the permanent opt out is to commence on B day and the Health Board, despite using its reasonable endeavours, has failed to find an alternative provider to take on the provision of the additional service from that day, it must notify the contractor in writing of this fact at least one month before B day, in which case the contractor is to continue to provide the additional service until C day unless at least one month before C day it

receives a notice from the Health Board under sub-paragraph (11) that it has applied to the assessment panel under sub-paragraph (10) seeking the approval of the assessment panel to a decision to refuse a permanent opt out or to postpone the commencement of a permanent opt out until after C day.

(9) As soon as is reasonably practicable and in any event within 7 days of the date on which the Health Board served a notice under sub-paragraph (8), the Health Board must enter into discussions with the contractor concerning the support that the Health Board may give to the contractor or other changes which the Health Board or the contractor may make in relation to the provision of the additional service until C day.

(10) A Health Board may, if it considers that there are exceptional circumstances, make an application to the assessment panel for approval of a decision to—

(a) refuse a permanent opt out; or

(b) postpone the commencement of a permanent opt out until after C day.

(11) As soon as practicable after making an application under sub-paragraph (10) to the assessment panel, the Health Board must notify the contractor in writing that it has made such an application.

(12) The Health Board must ensure that an assessment panel is appointed by another Health Board as soon as is practicable to consider and determine whether or not to approve the Health Board's proposed decision to refuse a permanent opt out or to postpone the commencement of a permanent opt out until after C day.

(13) The Health Board must provide the assessment panel with such information as the assessment panel may reasonably require to enable it to reach a determination.

(14) On receiving an application under sub-paragraph (10) for approval of a decision to refuse a permanent opt out, the assessment panel must—

(a) approve the Health Board's application;

(b) reject the Health Board's application, but nonetheless recommend a different date for the commencement of the permanent opt out which may be later than C day; or

(c) reject the Health Board's application.

(15) On receiving an application under sub-paragraph (10) for approval of a decision to postpone the commencement of a permanent opt out until after C day, the assessment panel must—

(a) approve the Health Board's application;

(b) reject the Health Board's application, but nonetheless recommend—

(i) that the permanent opt out commence on an earlier date to that proposed by the Health Board in its application; or

(ii) that the permanent opt out be refused; or

(c) reject the Health Board's application.

(16) The assessment panel must notify the Health Board and the contractor in writing of its decision under sub-paragraph (14) or (15) as soon as is practicable, including reasons for its decision.

(17) Where the assessment panel—

(a) approves a decision to refuse an opt out under sub-paragraph (14)(a); or

(b) recommends that a permanent opt out be refused under sub-paragraph (15)(b)(ii),

the Health Board must notify the contractor in writing that the contractor may not opt out of the additional service.

(18) Where a Health Board notifies a contractor under sub-paragraph (17), the contractor may not serve a preliminary opt out notice in respect of that additional service for a period of twelve months beginning with the date of service of the Health Board's notice under sub-paragraph (17) unless there has been a change in the circumstances of the contractor in relation to its ability to deliver services under the contract.

(19) Where the assessment panel—

(a) recommends a different date for the commencement of the permanent opt out under sub-paragraph (14)(b);

(b) approves a Health Board's application to postpone a permanent opt out under sub-paragraph (15)(a); or

(c) recommends an earlier date to that proposed by the Health Board in its application under sub-paragraph (15)(b)(i),

the Health Board must in accordance with the decision of the assessment panel notify the contractor in writing of its decision and the notice must specify the date of the commencement of the permanent opt out.

(20) Where the assessment panel rejects the Health Board's application under sub-paragraph (14)(c) or (15)(c), the Health Board must notify the contractor in writing that there will be a permanent opt out, and the permanent opt out must commence on C day or 28 days after the date of service of the Health Board's notice, whichever is the later.

(21) If the assessment panel has not reached a decision on the Health Board's application under sub-paragraph (10) before C day, the contractor's obligation to provide the additional service will continue until a notice is served on the contractor by the Health Board under sub-paragraph (19) or (20).

(22) Nothing in sub-paragraphs (1) to (21) above prevents the contractor and the Health Board from agreeing a different date for the termination of the contractor's duty under the contract to provide the additional service and, accordingly, varying the contract in accordance with paragraph 94(1) of schedule 6.

(23) The permanent opt out takes effect at 0800 hours on the relevant day unless—

(a) the day is not a working day, in which case the opt out will take effect on the next working day at 0800 hours; or

(b) the Health Board and the contractor agree a different day or time.

(24) Any decision or determination by the assessment panel for the purposes of this paragraph may be reached by a majority.

Informing patients of opt-outs

4.—(1) Prior to any opt out taking effect, the Health Board and the contractor must discuss how to inform patients of the proposed opt out.

(2) The contractor must, if requested by the Health Board inform the contractor's registered patients of an opt out and the arrangements made for them to receive the additional service by—

(a) placing a notice in the practice's waiting room; or

(b) including the information in the practice leaflet.

(3) In this paragraph "opt out" means, a permanent opt out or a temporary opt out.

SCHEDULE 3 Regulation 24

MINIMUM STANDARDS FOR PRACTICE PREMISES

1. The contractor must ensure that it meets minimum standards for its practice premises which are that—

(a) the contractor complies with any obligations under the Health and Safety at Work etc. Act 1974(**a**) (and provision made under that Act) and the Equality Act 2010(**b**) in relation to—

  (i) the design or construction of the practice premises; and

  (ii) the approach or access to the practice premises,

  which the contractor has to its own members (where applicable), staff, contractors and to persons to whom it provides primary medical services, including taking such steps as are reasonable to—

   (aa) provide for ease of access to the practice premises and ease of movement within the practice premises for all users of the practice premises (including wheelchair users);

   (bb) provide adequate sound and visual systems for the hearing and visually impaired; and

   (cc) remove barriers to the employment of disabled people;

(b) there are adequate facilities for the elderly and young children, including nappy-changing and feeding facilities;

(c) there are adequate lavatory and hand hygiene facilities for all persons on the practice premises which meet current infection control standards;

(d) there is such equipment as is necessary to enable the contractor to properly perform appropriate clinical services in the consultation rooms and treatment areas;

(e) the practice have arrangements for instrument decontamination that comply with any national guidelines for instrument decontamination published by the Scottish Ministers from time to time which apply to primary care in accordance with paragraph 119 of schedule 6;

(f) subject to sub-paragraph (g), consulting rooms and treatment areas are properly equipped for use by practitioners working in the practice, including—

  (i) adequate arrangements to ensure the privacy of consultations; and

  (ii) patients have personal privacy when dressing or undressing, either in a separate examination room or in a screened-off area around an examination couch within the relevant consulting rooms and treatment areas;

(g) in the case of branch surgeries where the contractor provides outlying consultation facilities in premises usually used for other purposes, and these outlying consultation facilities meet with the approval of the Health Board, the standards set out in sub-paragraph (f) do not apply in relation to the outlying consultation facilities;

(h) the access arrangements for the practice premises are convenient for all users;

(i) there are washbasins connected to running hot and cold water (ideally distributed through elbow, knee or sensor operated taps) in all consulting rooms and treatment areas, or, if this is not possible, then in immediately adjacent rooms;

(**a**) 1974 c.37.
(**b**) 2010 c.15.

(j) there are adequate internal waiting areas with—

  (i) enough seating to meet all normal requirements, either in the reception area or elsewhere; and

  (ii) a facility for patients to communicate confidentially with reception staff, including by telephone;

(k) there are adequate standards of lighting, heating and ventilation;

(l) the fittings and furniture of the practice premises are in good repair and (when being used for the provision of primary medical services) clean and hygienic;

(m) there are arrangements for the storage and disposal of clinical waste and that these arrangements comply with the legislative requirements and national guidance in place from time to time in accordance with paragraph 119 of schedule 6;

(n) there are, in the practice premises, arrangements for adequate fire precautions designed in accordance with the Building (Scotland) Regulations 2004(**a**) and agreed with the local fire authority, including provision for safe exit from the practice premises;

(o) there is adequate security for drugs, records, prescription pads and pads of doctors' statements; and

(p) if the premises are to be used for minor surgery or the treatment of minor injuries, there are necessary facilities and equipment to enable the proper performance of these procedures in the practice premises.

(**a**) S.S.I. 2004/406 as amended by S.S.I. 2006/534, S.S.I. 2008/310, S.S.I. 2009/119, S.S.I. 2010/32, S.S.I. 2011/120, S.S.I. 2011/211, S.S.I. 2012/209, S.S.I. 2013/143, S.S.I. 2014/219, S.I. 2014/1638, S.S.I. 2015/218, S.S.I. 2016/70, S.S.I. 2016/71 and S.S.I. 2017/188.

SCHEDULE 4

Regulation 25

LIST OF PRESCRIBED MEDICAL CERTIFICATES

Description of medical certificate	*Enactment under or for the purpose of which certificate required*	*Alternative provider*
1. To support a claim or to obtain payment either personally or by proxy; to prove incapacity to work or for self-support for the purposes of an award by the Secretary of State; or to enable proxy to draw pensions etc.	Naval and Marine Pay and Pensions Act 1865(**a**) Air Force (Constitution) Act 1917(**b**) Pensions (Navy, Army, Air Force and Mercantile Marine) Act 1939(**c**) Personal Injuries (Emergency Provisions) Act 1939(**d**) Pensions (Mercantile Marine) Act 1942(**e**) Polish Resettlement Act 1947(**f**) Social Security Administration Act 1992(**g**) Social Security Contributions and Benefits Act 1992(**h**)	
	Social Security Act 1998(**i**)	Health care professional(**j**)
2. To establish pregnancy for the purpose of obtaining welfare foods.	Section 13 of the Social Security Act 1988 (schemes for distribution etc. of welfare foods)(**k**)	Registered midwife or registered nurse(**l**)

(**a**) 1865 c.73.
(**b**) 1917 c.51.
(**c**) 1939 c.83.
(**d**) 1939 c.82.
(**e**) 1942 c.26.
(**f**) 1947 c.19.
(**g**) 1992 c.5.
(**h**) 1992 c.4.
(**i**) 1998 c.14 ("the 1998 Act").
(**j**) The Secretary of State and the First-tier Tribunal may, before making a decision on a benefit claim refer the claimant to a "health care professional" approved by the Secretary of State for an examination and report under sections 19 and 20 of the 1998 Act. For these purposes a health care professional has the same meaning as in these Regulations: section 39 of the 1998 Act. Section 19 of the 1998 Act was amended by Part 1 of schedule 10 of Social Security Contributions (Transfer of Functions etc) Act 1999 (c.2) ("the 1999 Act") and section 62(2) of the Welfare Reform Act 2007 (c.5) ("the 2007 Act"). Section 20 of the 1998 Act was amended by Part 1 of schedule 10 of the 1999 Act, section 62(3) of the 2007 Act and S.I. 2008/2833. Section 39 of the 1998 Act was relevantly amended by section 62(5) of the 2007 Act.
(**k**) 1988 c.7. Section 13 was substituted by section 185 of the Health and Social Care (Community Health and Standards) Act 2003 (c.43).
(**l**) Paragraphs 2 and 5 of S.I. 2005/3262 require claims to be signed by a health professional. "Health professional" is defined in regulation 2 of S.I. 2005/3262 as a registered medical practitioner, registered nurse or registered midwife.

Description of medical certificate	Enactment under or for the purpose of which certificate required	Alternative provider
3. To secure registration of still-birth.	Section 21 of the Registration of Births, Deaths and Marriages (Scotland) Act 1965 (special provision as to registration of still-birth)(**a**)	Registered midwife
4. To establish unfitness for jury service.	Criminal Procedure (Scotland) Act 1995(**b**) Court Of Session Act 1988(**c**)	
5. To support late application for reinstatement in civil employment or notification of non-availability to take up employment owing to sickness.	Reserve Forces (Safeguard of Employment) Act 1985(**d**)	
6. To enable a person to be registered as an absent voter on grounds of physical incapacity.	Paragraph 3(3) (b) of schedule 4 of Representation of the People Act 2000(**e**)	(a) a registered nurse; (b) a registered dentist; (c) a registered dispensing optician or a registered optometrist; (d) a registered pharmacist; (e) a registered osteopath; (f) a registered chiropractor (g) a Christian Science practitioner;

(**a**) 1965 c.49. Section 21 was amended by section 24, paragraphs 12 and 13 of schedule 7 and schedule 8 of the Nurses, Midwives and Health Visitors Act 1979 (c.36), section 40 of the Local Electoral Administration and Registration Services (Scotland) Act 2006 (asp 14) and sections 26, 27 and paragraph 3 of schedule 2 of the Certification of Death (Scotland) Act 2011 (asp 11).
(**b**) 1995 c.46.
(**c**) 1988 c.36.
(**d**) 1985 c.17.
(**e**) 2000 c.2 ("the 2000 Act"). Paragraph 3(3)(b) of schedule 4 was amended by paragraph 137 of schedule 1 of the Electoral Administration Act 2006 (c.22) and section 34(5) of the Local Electoral Administration and Registration Services (Scotland) Act 2006. Those able to attest and sign an application under paragraph 3(3)(b) of schedule 4 of the 2000 Act are listed in regulation 53(2) of S.I. 2001/497, as amended by S.I. 2002/253, S.I. 2002/254, S.I. 2007/925, S.I. 2009/1182, S.I. 2010/231, S.I. 2011/2581 and S.I. 2012/1479.

Description of medical certificate	Enactment under or for the purpose of which certificate required	Alternative provider	
		(h)	a person registered as a member of a profession to which the Health and Social Work Professions Order 2001(**a**) for the time being extends, other than social worker;
		(i)	The manager of a care home service registered under a registered care home under Part 5 of the Public Services Reform (Scotland) Act 2010(**b**);
		(j)	the warden of premises forming one of a group of premises provided for persons of pensionable age or disabled persons for which there is a resident warden, where the applicant states that he resides in such premises;

(**a**) S.I. 2002/254, as retitled by section 213(6) of the Health and Social Care Act 2012 (c.7). Article 5 was amended by S.I. 2009/1182. The title of this Order is the Health and Social Work Profession Order 2002 but it is cited as the Health and Social Work Profession Order 2001 in accordance with section 213(4) of the Health and Social Care Act 2012.
(**b**) 2010 asp 8. "Care home service" is defined in paragraph 2 of schedule 12 of that Act.

Description of medical certificate	Enactment under or for the purpose of which certificate required	Alternative provider	
		(k)	a hospital manager (or a person on behalf of a manager) within the meaning of section 329 of the Mental Health (Care and Treatment) (Scotland) Act 2003(**a**); or
		(l)	a person registered as a social worker
7. To support applications for certificates conferring exemption from charges in respect of drugs, medicines and appliances.	National Health Service (Scotland) Act 1978(**b**) National Health Service (Free Prescriptions and Charges for Drugs and Appliances) (Scotland) Regulations 2011(**c**)	Registered midwife or health care professional	
8. To support a claim by or on behalf of a severely mentally impaired person for exemption from liability to pay council tax or eligibility for a discount in respect of the amount of council tax payable.	Paragraph 2(1) (b) of schedule 1 of the Local Government Finance Act 1992(**d**)		
10. To secure certification of cause of death.	Section 24 of the Registration of Births, Deaths and Marriages (Scotland) Act 1965 (certificate of cause of death)(**e**)		

(**a**) 2003 asp 13. "Hospital" and "Managers" (in relation to a hospital) are defined in section 329 of that Act. Section 329 was relevantly amended by S.S.I. 2011/211.
(**b**) 1978 c.29.
(**c**) S.S.I. 2011/550.
(**d**) 1992 c.14.
(**e**) Section 24 was amended by section 42(4) of the Local Electoral Administrations and Registration Services (Scotland) Act 2006 and section 26 and paragraph 4 of schedule 2 of the Certification of Death (Scotland) Act 2011.

SCHEDULE 5

Regulation 28

FEES AND CHARGES

1. The contractor may demand or accept a fee or other remuneration—

(a) from any statutory body for services rendered for the purposes of that body's statutory functions;

(b) from any body, employer or school for a routine medical examination of persons for whose welfare the body, employer or school is responsible, or an examination of such persons for the purpose of advising the body, employer or school of any administrative action they might take;

(c) for treatment which is not primary medical services or otherwise required to be provided under the contract and which is given—

   (i) pursuant to the provisions of section 57 of the Act(**a**) (accommodation and services for private patients); or

   (ii) in accommodation provided by a care home service which is not providing services under the Act,

   if, in either case, the person providing the treatment is serving on the staff of a hospital providing services under the Act as a specialist providing treatment of the kind the patient requires and if, within 7 days of giving the treatment, the contractor or the person providing the treatment supplies the Health Board, on a form provided by it for the purpose, with such information about the treatment as it may require;

(d) under section 158 of the Road Traffic Act 1988 (payment for emergency treatment of traffic casualties)(**b**);

(e) when the contractor treats a patient under regulation 28(3), in which case the contractor is entitled to demand and accept a reasonable fee (recoverable in certain circumstances under regulation 28(4)) for any treatment given, if the contractor gives the patient a receipt;

(f) for attending and examining (but not otherwise treating) a patient—

   (i) at the patient's request at a police station in connection with possible criminal proceedings against the patient;

   (ii) at the request of a commercial, educational or not-for-profit organisation for the purpose of creating a medical report or certificate; or

   (iii) for the purpose of creating a medical report required in connection with an actual or potential claim for compensation by the patient;

(g) for treatment consisting of an immunisation for which no remuneration is payable by the Health Board and which is requested in connection with travel abroad;

(h) for prescribing or providing drugs, medicines or appliances (including a collection of such drugs, medicines and appliances in the form of a travel kit) which a patient requires to have in their possession solely in anticipation of the onset of an ailment or occurrence of an injury while they are outside the United Kingdom but for which they are not requiring treatment when the medicine is prescribed;

(i) for a medical examination—

   (i) to enable a decision to be made as to whether or not it is inadvisable on medical grounds for a person to wear a seat belt; or

---

(**a**) Section 57 was substituted by section 7 of the Health and Medicines Act 1988 (c.49), and amended by paragraph 19(1) of schedule 9 and paragraph 1 of schedule 10 of the National Health Service and Community Care Act 1990 (c.19).

(**b**) 1988 c.52. Section 158 was amended by section 20(2) of the Community Care and Health (Scotland) Act 2002 (asp 5).

      (ii) for the purpose of creating a report—
           (aa) relating to a road traffic accident or criminal assault; or
           (bb) that offers an opinion as to whether a patient is fit to travel; or
(j) for prescribing or providing drugs or medicines for malaria chemoprophylaxis.

SCHEDULE 6

Regulation 30

OTHER CONTRACTUAL TERMS

PART 1

PROVISION OF SERVICES

Premises

1. Subject to any plan which is included in the contract pursuant to regulation 21(3), the contractor must ensure that the premises used for the provision of services under the contract are—
   (a) suitable for the delivery of those services; and
   (b) sufficient to meet the reasonable needs of the contractor's patients.

Telephone services

2.—(1) The contractor must not be a party to any contract or other arrangement under which the number for telephone services to be used—
   (a) by patients to contact the practice for any purpose related to the contract; or
   (b) by any other person to contact the practice in relation to services provided as part of the health service,

starts with the digits 087, or 09 or consists of a personal number, unless the service is provided free to the caller.

(2) In this paragraph, "personal number" means a telephone number which starts with the number 070 followed by a further 8 digits.

Attendance at practice premises

3.—(1) The contractor must take steps to ensure that any patient who—
   (a) has not previously made an appointment; and
   (b) attends at the practice premises during the normal hours for essential services,

is provided with such services by an appropriate health care professional during that surgery period except in the circumstances specified in sub-paragraph (2).

(2) The circumstances referred to in sub-paragraph (1) are that—
   (a) it is more appropriate for the patient to be referred elsewhere for services under the Act; or
   (b) the patient is then offered an appointment to attend again within a time which is appropriate and reasonable having regard to all the circumstances and the patient's health would not thereby be jeopardised.

Attendance outside practice premises

4.—(1) In the case of a patient whose medical condition is such that in the reasonable opinion of the contractor—
   (a) attendance on the patient is required; and
   (b) it would be inappropriate for the patient to attend at the practice premises,

the contractor must provide services to that patient at whichever in its judgement is the most appropriate of the places set out in sub-paragraph (2).

(2) The places referred to in sub-paragraph (1) are—

- (a) the place recorded in the patient's medical records as being the patient's last home address;
- (b) such other place as the contractor has informed the patient and the Health Board is the place where the contractor has agreed to visit and treat the patient; or
- (c) some other place in the contractor's practice area.

(3) Nothing in this paragraph prevents the contractor from—

- (a) arranging for the referral of a patient without first seeing the patient, in a case where the medical condition of that patient makes that course of action appropriate; or
- (b) visiting the patient in circumstances where this paragraph does not place it under an obligation to do so.

Newly registered patients

5.—(1) Where a patient has been—

- (a) accepted on a contractor's list of patients under paragraph 12; or
- (b) assigned to that list by the Health Board,

the contractor must, in addition to and without prejudice to its other obligations in respect of that patient under the contract, invite the patient to participate in a consultation either at the contractor's practice premises or, if the medical condition of the patient so warrants, at one of the places referred to in paragraph 4(2).

(2) An invitation under sub-paragraph (1) must be issued within six months of the date of the acceptance of the patient on, or their assignment to, the contractor's list and may offer the patient a consultation with—

- (a) the contractor;
- (b) a medical practitioner employed or engaged by the contractor; or
- (c) a healthcare professional employed or engaged by the contractor.

(3) Where a patient (or, where appropriate, in the case of a patient who is a child, the child's parent) agrees to participate in a consultation mentioned in sub-paragraph (1), with a person mentioned in sub-paragraph (2), that person must, in the course of that consultation make such inquiries and undertake such examinations as appear to him or her to be appropriate in all the circumstances.

Clinical reports

6.—(1) Where the contractor provides any clinical services, other than under a private arrangement, to a patient who is not on the contractor's list of patients, the contractor must, as soon as reasonably practicable, provide a clinical report relating to the consultation, and any treatment provided, to the Health Board.

(2) The Health Board must send any report received under sub-paragraph (1)—

- (a) to the person with whom the patient is registered for the provision of essential services or their equivalent; or
- (b) if the person referred to in paragraph (a) is not known to it, to the Health Board in whose area the patient is resident.

Storage of vaccines

7. The contractor must ensure that—

(a) all vaccines are stored in a pharmaceutical refrigerator, designed for the purpose of storing vaccines or medicines, in accordance with the manufacturer's instructions;

(b) all refrigerators in which vaccines are stored have a calibrated maximum/minimum digital thermometer on which readings are taken on all working days to ensure the temperature remains within the specified range of +2°C to +8°C; and

(c) it has regard to Health Protection Scotland guidance on Vaccine Storage and Handling(**a**).

Infection control

8. The contractor must ensure that it has appropriate arrangements for infection control and decontamination.

Duty of co-operation in relation to additional and enhanced services

9.—(1) A contractor which does not provide to its registered patients or to persons whom it has accepted as temporary residents—

(a) a particular additional service; or

(b) a particular enhanced service;

must comply with the requirements specified in sub-paragraph (2).

(2) The requirements referred to in sub-paragraph (1) are that the contractor must—

(a) co-operate, insofar as it is reasonable, with any person responsible for the provision of that service or those services; and

(b) comply in core hours with any reasonable request for information from such a person or from the Health Board relating to the provision of that service or those services.

Duty of co-operation in relation to additional and enhanced services

10. Where a contractor is to cease to be required to provide to its patients—

(a) a particular additional service; or

(b) a particular enhanced service,

it must comply with any reasonable request for information relating to the provision of that service or those services made by the Health Board or by any person with whom the Board intends to enter into a contract for the provision of such services.

PART 2

PATIENTS

List of patients

11. The Health Board must prepare and keep up to date a list of the patients—

(a) who have been accepted by the contractor for inclusion in its list of patients under paragraph 12 and who have not subsequently been removed from that list under paragraphs 16 to 24; and

---

(**a**) The current version of the guidance is version 3.0, December 2017 and can be found at http://www.hps.scot.nhs.uk/resourcedocument.aspx?id=6330

(b) who have been assigned to the contractor under paragraph 29 or 30 and whose assignment has not subsequently been rescinded.

Application for inclusion in a list of patients

12.—(1) The contractor may, if its list of patients is open, accept an application for inclusion in its list of patients made by or on behalf of any person whether or not resident in its practice area or included, at the time of that application, in the list of patients of another contractor or provider of primary medical services.

(2) The contractor may, if its list of patients is closed, only accept an application for inclusion in its list of patients from a person who is an immediate family member of a registered patient whether or not resident in its practice area or included, at the time of that application, in the list of patients of another contractor or provider of primary medical services.

(3) Subject to sub-paragraph (4), an application for inclusion in a contractor's list of patients must be made by delivering to the practice premises an application signed by the applicant or a person authorised by the applicant to sign on the applicant's behalf.

(4) An application may be made—

(a) on behalf of any child—

   (i) by either parent, or in the absence of both parents, the guardian or other adult person who has care of the child;

   (ii) by a person duly authorised by a local authority, where the child is in the care of a local authority under the Children (Scotland) Act 1995(**a**); or

   (iii) by a person duly authorised by a voluntary organisation, by which the child is being accommodated under the provisions of that Act; or

(b) on behalf of any adult who is incapable of making such an application, or authorising such an application to be made on their behalf, by the primary carer of that person or by a person authorised under the Adults with Incapacity (Scotland) Act 2000(**b**) to act on the patient's behalf.

(5) A contractor which accepts an application for inclusion in its list of patients must notify the Health Board in writing as soon as possible.

(6) On receipt of a notice under sub-paragraph (5), the Health Board must—

(a) include that person in the contractor's list of patients from the date on which the notice is received; and

(b) notify the applicant (or, in the case of a child or incapable adult, the person making the application on their behalf) of the acceptance.

Temporary residents

13.—(1) The contractor may, if its list of patients is open, accept a person as a temporary resident provided it is satisfied that the person is—

(a) temporarily resident away from the person's normal place of residence and is not being provided with essential services (or their equivalent) under any other arrangement in the locality where the person is temporarily residing; or

(b) moving from place to place and not for the time being resident in any place.

(2) For the purposes of sub-paragraph (1), a person is regarded as temporarily resident in a place if, when the person arrives in that place, the person intends to stay there for more than 24 hours but not more than three months.

(**a**) 1995 c.36.
(**b**) 2000 asp 4.

(3) A contractor which wishes to terminate its responsibility for a person accepted as a temporary resident before the end of—

(a) three months; or

(b) such shorter period for which it agreed to accept the person as a patient,

must notify the person either orally or in writing and its responsibility for that patient will cease 7 days after the date on which the notification was given.

(4) At the end of three months, or on such earlier date as its responsibility for the temporary resident has come to an end, the contractor must notify the Health Board in writing of any person whom it accepted as a temporary resident.

Refusal of application for inclusion in the list of patients or for acceptance as a temporary resident

14.—(1) The contractor may only refuse an application made under paragraph 12 or 13 if it has reasonable grounds for doing so which do not relate to the applicant's race, gender, social class, age, religion, sexual orientation, appearance, disability or medical condition.

(2) The reasonable grounds referred to in paragraph (1) may, in the case of applications made under paragraph 12, include the ground that the applicant does not live in the contractor's practice area.

(3) A contractor which refuses an application made under paragraph 12 or 13 must, within 14 days of its decision, notify the applicant (or, in the case of a child or incapable adult, the person making the application on their behalf) in writing of the refusal and the reason for it.

(4) The contractor must keep a written record of refusals of applications made under paragraph 12 and of the reasons for them and must make this record available to the Health Board on request.

Patient preference of practitioner

15.—(1) Where the contractor has accepted an application for inclusion in its list of patients, it must—

(a) notify the patient (or, in the case of a child or incapable adult, the person who made the application on their behalf) of the patient's right to express a preference to receive services from a particular performer or class of performer either generally or in relation to any particular condition; and

(b) record in writing any such preference expressed by or on behalf of the patient.

(2) The contractor must endeavour to comply with any reasonable preference expressed under sub-paragraph (1) but need not do so if the preferred performer—

(a) has reasonable grounds for refusing to provide services to the patient; or

(b) does not routinely perform the service in question within the practice.

Removal from the list at the request of the patient

16.—(1) The contractor must notify the Health Board in writing of any request for removal from its list of patients received from a registered patient.

(2) Where the Health Board—

(a) receives notification from the contractor under sub-paragraph (1); or

(b) receives a request from the patient to be removed from the contractor's list of patients,

it must remove that person from the contractor's list of patients.

(3) A removal in accordance with sub-paragraph (2) will take effect on whichever is the earlier of the following dates—

(a) on the date on which the Health Board received notification of the registration of the person with another provider of essential services (or their equivalent); or

(b) 14 days after the date on which the notification or request made under sub-paragraph (1) or (2) respectively is received by the Health Board.

(4) The Health Board must, as soon as practicable, notify in writing—

(a) the patient; and

(b) the contractor,

that the patient's name will be or has been removed from the contractor's list of patients on the date referred to in sub-paragraph (3).

(5) In this paragraph and in paragraphs 17(1)(b) and (10), 18(6) and (7), 20 and 23, a reference to a request received from or advice, information or notification required to be given to a patient includes a request received from or advice, information or notification required to be given to—

(a) in the case of a patient who is a child, a parent or other person referred to in paragraph 12(4)(a); or

(b) in the case of an adult patient who is incapable of making the relevant request or receiving the relevant advice, information or notification, a relative or the primary carer of the patient.

Removal from the list at the request of the contractor

17.—(1) Subject to paragraph 18, a contractor which has reasonable grounds for wishing a patient to be removed from its list of patients which do not relate to the applicant's race, gender, social class, age, religion, sexual orientation, appearance, disability or medical condition must—

(a) notify the Health Board in writing that it wishes to have the patient removed; and

(b) subject to sub-paragraph (2), notify the patient of its specific reasons for requesting removal.

(2) Where, in the reasonable opinion of the contractor—

(a) the circumstances of the removal are such that it is not appropriate for a more specific reason to be given; and

(b) there has been an irrevocable breakdown in the relationship between the patient and the contractor,

the reason given under sub-paragraph (1) may consist of a statement that there has been such a breakdown.

(3) Except in the circumstances described in sub-paragraph (4), a contractor may only request a removal under sub-paragraph (1) if, within the period of twelve months prior to the date of its request to the Health Board it has—

(a) warned the patient that the patient is at risk of removal and explained to the patient the reasons for this; and

(b) confirmed that the Health Board has agreed to the removal ground mentioned in sub-paragraph (1).

(4) The circumstances referred to in sub-paragraph (3) are that—

(a) the reason for the removal relates to a change of address;

(b) the contractor has reasonable grounds for believing that the issue of such a warning would—

(i) be harmful to the physical or mental health of the patient; or

(ii) put at risk the safety of the persons specified in sub-paragraph (5); or

(c) it is, in the opinion of the contractor, not otherwise reasonably practicable for a warning to be given.

(5) The persons referred to in sub-paragraph (4) are—

(a) in the case of a contract with an individual medical practitioner, that practitioner;

(b) in the case of a contract with a partnership, a partner in that partnership;

(c) in the case of a contract with a limited liability partnership, a member of that limited liability partnership;

(d) in the case of a contract with a company, a member of that company;

(e) a member of the contractor's staff;

(f) a person engaged by the contractor to perform or assist in the performance of services under the contract; or

(g) any other person present—

    (i) on the practice premises; or

    (ii) in the place where services are being provided to the patient under the contract.

(6) The contractor must record in writing—

(a) the date of any warning given in accordance with sub-paragraph (3) and the reasons for giving such a warning as explained to the patient; or

(b) the reason why no such warning was given.

(7) The contractor must keep a written record of removals under this paragraph which includes—

(a) the reason for removal given to the patient;

(b) the circumstances of the removal; and

(c) in cases where sub-paragraph (2) applies, the grounds for a more specific reason not being appropriate,

and must make this record available to the Health Board on request.

(8) A removal requested in accordance with sub-paragraph (1) will, subject to sub-paragraph (9) take effect from whichever is the earlier of the following dates—

(a) the date on which the Health Board receives notification of the registration of the person with another provider of essential services (or their equivalent); or

(b) the eighth day after the Health Board receives the notice referred to in sub-paragraph (1)(a).

(9) Where, on the date on which the removal would take effect under sub-paragraph (8), the contractor is treating the patient at intervals of less than 7 days, the contractor must notify the Health Board in writing of the fact and the removal will take effect on whichever is the earlier of the following dates—

(a) on the eighth day after the Health Board receives notification from the contractor that the person no longer needs such treatment; or

(b) on the date on which the Health Board receives notification of the registration of the person with another provider of essential services (or their equivalent).

(10) The Health Board must notify in writing—

(a) the patient; and

(b) the contractor,

that the patient's name has been or will be removed from the contractor's list of patients on the date referred to in sub-paragraph (8) or (9).

Removal from the list of patients who are violent

18.—(1) A contractor which wishes a patient to be removed from its list of patients with immediate effect on the grounds that—

(a) the patient has committed an act of violence against any of the persons specified in sub-paragraph (2) or behaved in such a way that any such person has feared for that person's own safety; and

(b) the contractor has reported the incident to the police or the Procurator Fiscal, must notify the Health Board in accordance with sub-paragraph (3).

(2) The persons referred to in sub-paragraph (1) are—

(a) in the case of a contract with an individual medical practitioner, that practitioner;

(b) in the case of a contract with a partnership, a partner in that partnership;

(c) in the case of a contract with a limited liability partnership, a member of that limited liability partnership;

(d) in the case of a contract with a company, a member of that company;

(e) a member of the contractor's staff;

(f) a person engaged by the contractor to perform or assist in the performance of services under the contract; or

(g) any other person present—

(i) on the practice premises; or

(ii) in the place where services were provided to the patient under the contract.

(3) Notification under sub-paragraph (1) may be given by any means including telephone and must be confirmed in writing within 7 days (and for this purpose transmission by electronic means is not a written one).

(4) The Health Board must acknowledge in writing receipt of a request from the contractor under sub-paragraph (1).

(5) A removal requested in accordance with sub-paragraph (1) will take effect at the time that the contractor—

(a) makes the telephone call to the Health Board; or

(b) sends or delivers the notification to the Health Board.

(6) Where, pursuant to this paragraph, the contractor has notified the Health Board that it wishes to have a patient removed from the contractor's list of patients with immediate effect, it must inform the patient concerned unless—

(a) it is not reasonably practicable for it to do so; or

(b) it has reasonable grounds for believing that to do so would—

(i) be harmful to the physical or mental health of the patient; or

(ii) put at risk the safety of one or more of the persons specified in sub-paragraph (2).

(7) Where the Health Board has removed a patient from the contractor's list of patients in accordance with sub-paragraph (5), it must give written notice of the removal to that patient.

(8) Where a patient is removed from the contractor's list of patients in accordance with this paragraph, the contractor must record in the patient's medical records that the patient has been removed under this paragraph and the circumstances leading to the patient's removal.

Removals from the list of patients registered elsewhere

19.—(1) The Health Board must remove a patient from the contractor's list of patients if—

(a) the patient has subsequently been registered with another provider of essential services (or their equivalent) in the area of the Health Board; or

(b) it has received notice from another Health Board, Local Health Board, the National Health Service Commissioning Board(a), or Regional Health and Social Care Board, that the patient has subsequently been registered with a provider of essential services (or their equivalent) outside the area of the Health Board.

(a) Established under section 1H of the National Health Service Act 2006 (c.41). Section 1H was inserted by section 9(1) of the Health and Social Care Act 2012 (c.7) and was amended by S.I. 2012/1831.

(2) A removal in accordance with sub-paragraph (1) will take effect—

(a) on the date on which the Health Board receives notification of the registration of the person with the new provider; or

(b) with the consent of the Health Board, on such other date as has been agreed between the contractor and the new provider.

(3) The Health Board must notify the contractor in writing of patients removed from its list of patients under sub-paragraph (1).

Removals from the list of patients who have moved

20.—(1) Subject to sub-paragraph (2), where the Health Board is satisfied that a person on the contractor's list of patients has moved and no longer resides in that contractor's practice area, the Board must—

(a) inform that patient and the contractor that the contractor is no longer obliged to visit and treat the person;

(b) advise the patient in writing either to obtain the contractor's agreement to the continued inclusion of the person on its list of patients or to apply for registration with another provider of essential services (or their equivalent); and

(c) inform the patient that if, after the expiry of 30 days from the date of the letter of advice mentioned in paragraph (b), the patient has not acted in accordance with the advice and informed the Board accordingly, the Health Board will remove the patient from the contractor's list of patients.

(2) If, at the expiry of the period of 30 days referred to in sub-paragraph (1)(c), the Health Board has not been notified of the action taken, it must remove the patient from the contractor's list of patients and inform the patient and the contractor accordingly.

Removals from the list of patients who have moved

21. Where the address of a patient who is on the contractor's list of patients is no longer known to the Health Board, the Health Board must—

(a) give the contractor notice in writing that it intends, at the end of the period of six months commencing with the date of the notice, to remove the patient from the contractor's list of patients; and

(b) at the end of that period, remove the patient from the contractor's list of patients unless, within that period, the contractor satisfies the Health Board that it is still responsible for providing essential services to that patient.

Removals from the list of patients absent from the United Kingdom etc.

22.—(1) The Health Board must remove a patient from the contractor's list of patients where it receives notification that that patient—

(a) intends to be away from the United Kingdom for a period of at least three months;

(b) is in Her Majesty's Forces;

(c) has been absent from the United Kingdom for a period of more than three months; or

(d) has died.

(2) A removal in accordance with sub-paragraph (1) will take effect—

(a) in the cases referred to in sub-paragraph (1)(a) and (b) from the date of the departure or enlistment or the date on which the Health Board first receives notification of the departure or enlistment, whichever is the later; or

(b) in the cases referred to in sub-paragraph (1) (c) and (d) from the date on which the Health Board first receives notification of the absence or death.

(3) The Health Board must notify the contractor in writing of patients removed from its list of patients under sub-paragraph (1).

Removals from the list of patients accepted elsewhere as temporary residents

23.—(1) The Health Board must remove from the contractor's list of patients a patient who has been accepted as a temporary resident by another contractor or other provider of essential services (or their equivalent) where it is satisfied, after due inquiry—

    (a) that the person's stay in the place of temporary residence has exceeded three months; and

    (b) that the patient has not returned to the patient's normal place of residence or any other place within the contractor's practice area.

(2) The Health Board must notify in writing of a removal under sub-paragraph (1)—

    (a) the contractor; and

    (b) where practicable, the patient.

(3) A notification to the patient under sub-paragraph (2)(b) must inform the patient of—

    (a) the patient's entitlement to make arrangements for the provision to the patient of essential services (or their equivalent), including by the contractor by which the patient has been treated as a temporary resident; and

    (b) the name and address of the Health Board in whose area the patient is resident.

Removals from the list of pupils etc. of a school

24.—(1) Where the contractor provides essential services under the contract to persons on the grounds that they are pupils at or staff or residents of a school, the Health Board must remove from the contractor's list of patients any such persons who do not appear on particulars of persons who are pupils at or staff or residents of that school provided by that school.

(2) Where the Health Board has made a request to a school to provide the particulars mentioned in sub-paragraph (1) and has not received them, it must consult the contractor as to whether it should remove from its list of patients any persons appearing on that list as pupils at, or staff or residents of, that school.

(3) The Health Board must notify the contractor in writing of patients removed from its list of patients under sub-paragraph (1).

Termination of responsibility for patients not registered with the contractor

25.—(1) Where a contractor—

    (a) has received an application for the provision of medical services other than essential services—

        (i) from a person who is not included in its list of patients; or

        (ii) from a person whom the contractor has not accepted as a temporary resident; or

        (iii) on behalf of a person mentioned in (i) or (ii) above, from one of the persons specified in paragraph 12(4); and

    (b) has accepted that person as a patient for the provision of the service in question,

its responsibility for that patient will be terminated in one of the circumstances referred to in sub-paragraph (2).

(2) The circumstances referred to in sub-paragraph (1) are—

    (a) the patient informs the contractor that the patient no longer wishes it to be responsible for provision of the service in question;

    (b) in cases where the contractor has reasonable grounds for terminating its responsibility which do not relate to the person's race, gender, social class, age, religion, sexual orientation, appearance, disability or medical condition, the contractor informs the patient that it no longer wishes to be responsible for providing the patient with the service in question; or

(c) it comes to the notice of the contractor that the patient—

(i) no longer resides in the area for which the contractor has agreed to provide the service in question; or

(ii) is no longer included in the list of patients of another contractor to whose registered patients the contractor has agreed to provide that service.

(3) A contractor which wishes to terminate its responsibility for a patient under sub-paragraph (2)(b) must notify the patient of the termination and the reason for it.

(4) The contractor must keep a written record of terminations under this paragraph and of the reasons for them and must make this record available to the Health Board on request.

(5) A termination under sub-paragraph (2)(b) will take effect—

(a) from the date on which the notice is given where the grounds for termination are those specified in paragraph 18(1); or

(b) in all other cases, 14 days from the date on which the notice is given.

Closure of lists of patients

26.—(1) A contractor which wishes to close its list of patients must notify the Health Board in writing to that effect.

(2) Within a period of 28 days beginning with the date of receipt of the notification referred to in sub-paragraph (1), the Health Board must enter into discussions with the contractor concerning the support which the Health Board may give the contractor, or other changes which the Health Board or the contractor may make, which would enable the contractor to keep its list of patients open.

(3) In the discussions referred to in sub-paragraph (2), both parties must use reasonable endeavours to achieve the aim of keeping the contractor's list of patients open.

(4) The discussions mentioned in sub-paragraph (2) must be completed within a period of 3 months beginning with the date of the Health Board's receipt of the notification referred to in sub-paragraph (1), or within such longer period as the parties may agree.

(5) Notwithstanding the requirements mentioned in sub-paragraphs (2) and (4), the contractor may issue a closure notice to the Health Board which the Health Board must approve in accordance with sub-paragraph (13) if—

(a) the period of 28 days mentioned in sub-paragraph (2) has expired and the Health Board has not begun discussions with the contractor in accordance with sub-paragraph (2); or

(b) the 3 month period or such longer period as has been agreed in accordance with sub-paragraph (4) has expired and the Health Board has failed to complete the discussions mentioned in sub-paragraph (2).

(6) If, following the discussions mentioned in sub-paragraph (2), the Health Board and the contractor reach agreement that the contractor's list of patients should remain open, the Health Board must send full details of the agreement in writing to the contractor within a period of two weeks beginning with the date the agreement was reached.

(7) The Health Board and the contractor must comply with the terms of an agreement reached as mentioned in sub-paragraph (6).

(8) If, following the discussions mentioned in sub-paragraph (2)—

(a) the Health Board and the contractor reach agreement that the contractor's list of patients should close; or

(b) the Health Board and the contractor fail to reach agreement and the contractor still wishes to close the contractor's list of patients,

the contractor must send a closure notice to the Health Board.

(9) A closure notice mentioned in sub-paragraphs (5) or (8) must be submitted in the form specified in schedule 7, and must include the following details which (in a case falling within sub-paragraph (8)(a)) have been agreed between the parties or (in a case falling within sub-paragraph (8)(b)) are proposed by the contractor—

(a) the period of time (which may not exceed twelve months) for which the contractor's list of patients will be closed;

(b) the current number of the contractor's registered patients;

(c) the number of registered patients (lower than the current number of such patients, and expressed either in absolute terms or as a percentage of the number of such patients specified pursuant to paragraph (b)) which, if that number were reached, would trigger the re-opening of the contractor's list of patients;

(d) the number of registered patients (expressed either in absolute terms or as a percentage of the number of such patients specified pursuant to paragraph (b)) which, if that number were reached, would trigger the re-closure of the contractor's list of patients; and

(e) any withdrawal or reduction in provision of any additional or enhanced services which had previously been provided under the contract.

(10) The Health Board must, without delay, acknowledge receipt of the closure notice mentioned in sub-paragraphs (5) or (8) in writing to the contractor.

(11) Before the Health Board reaches a decision as to whether to approve or reject the closure notice mentioned in sub-paragraph (8) under sub-paragraph (14), the Health Board and the contractor may enter into further discussions concerning the details of the closure notice as specified in sub-paragraph (9), with a view to reaching agreement; and, in particular, if the parties are unable to reach agreement regarding the period of time for which the contractor's list of patients will be closed, that period will be twelve months.

(12) A contractor may not withdraw a closure notice mentioned in sub-paragraphs (5) or (8) for a period of three months beginning with the date on which the Health Board has received the notice, unless the Health Board has agreed otherwise in writing.

(13) Within a period of 14 days beginning with the date of the receipt of the closure notice mentioned in sub-paragraph (5), the Health Board must approve the closure notice and notify the contractor in writing as soon as possible.

(14) Within a period of 14 days beginning with the date of receipt of the closure notice mentioned in sub-paragraph (8), the Health Board must—

(a) approve the closure notice; or

(b) reject the closure notice,

and must notify the contractor of its decision in writing as soon as possible.

(15) Approval of a closure notice includes—

(a) where it is a closure notice mentioned in sub-paragraph (5), approval of the details specified in accordance with sub-paragraph (9); or

(b) where it is a closure notice mentioned in sub-paragraph (8) and approved under sub-paragraph (14)(a), approval of the details specified in accordance with sub-paragraph (9)(or, where those details are revised following discussions under sub-paragraph (11), approval of those details as so revised).

Approval of closure notice by the Health Board

27.—(1) If the Health Board approves the closure notice in accordance with paragraph 26(13) or paragraph 26(14)(a), the contractor must close its list of patients—

(a) with effect from a date agreed between the Health Board and the contractor; or

(b) if no such agreement has been reached, with effect from the date on which the contractor receives notification of the Health Board's decision to approve the closure notice.

(2) Subject to sub-paragraph (3), the contractor's list of patients is to remain closed for the period specified in the closure notice in accordance with paragraph 26(9)(a) (or, where a period of twelve months has been fixed in accordance with paragraph 26(11), for that period).

(3) The contractor's list of patients is to re-open before the expiry of the period mentioned in sub-paragraph (2) if—

(a) the number of the contractor's registered patients falls to the number specified in the closure notice in accordance with paragraph 26(9)(c); or

(b) the Health Board and the contractor agree that the list of patients should re-open.

(4) If the contractor's list of patients has re-opened pursuant to sub-paragraph (3)(a), it will nevertheless close again if, during the period specified in the closure notice in accordance with paragraph 26(9)(a) (or, where the period of twelve months specified in paragraph 26(11) applies, during that period) the number of the contractor's registered patients rises to the number specified in the closure notice in accordance with paragraph 26(9)(d).

(5) Except in cases where the contractor's list of patients is already open pursuant to sub-paragraph (3), the Health Board must notify the contractor in writing between 7 and 14 days before the expiry of the period of closure specified in sub-paragraph (2), confirming the date on which the contractor's list of patients will re-open.

(6) Where the details specified in the closure notice mentioned in paragraph 26(8) in accordance with paragraph 26(9) have been revised following discussions under paragraph 26(11), references in this paragraph to details specified in the closure notice are references to those details as so revised.

Rejection of closure notice by the Health Board

28.—(1) This regulation applies where the Health Board rejects the closure notice in accordance with paragraph 26(14)(b).

(2) The contractor and the Health Board may not refer the matter for determination in accordance with the NHS dispute resolution procedure (or, where applicable, commence court proceedings) until the assessment panel has given its determination in accordance with the following sub-paragraphs.

(3) The Health Board must ensure that an assessment panel is appointed by another Health Board as soon as is practicable to consider and determine whether the contractor should be permitted to close its list of patients, and if so, the terms on which the contractor should be permitted to do so.

(4) The Health Board must provide the assessment panel with such information as the assessment panel may reasonably require to enable the panel to reach a determination and must include in such information any written observations received from the contractor.

(5) At least one member of the assessment panel must visit the contractor before reaching a determination under sub-paragraph (6).

(6) Within the period of 28 days beginning with the date on which the Health Board rejected the closure notice, the assessment panel must—

(a) approve the list closure; or

(b) reject the list closure,

and must notify the Health Board and the contractor of its determination in writing as soon as possible.

(7) Where the assessment panel determines in accordance with sub-paragraph (6)(a) that the contractor's list of patients should close, it must specify—

(a) a date from which the closure is to take effect, which must be within a period of 7 days beginning with the date of the assessment panel's determination; and

(b) those details specified in paragraph 26(9).

(8) Subject to sub-paragraph (9), the contractor's list of patients is to remain closed for the period specified by the assessment panel in accordance with sub-paragraph (7)(b).

(9) The contractor's list of patients is to re-open before the expiry of the period mentioned in sub-paragraph (8) if—

- (a) the number of the contractor's registered patients falls to the number specified by the assessment panel in accordance with sub-paragraph (7)(b) as the number of registered patients which, if that number were reached, would trigger the re-opening of the contractor's list of patients; or
- (b) the Health Board and the contractor agree that the list of patients should re-open.

(10) If the contractor's list of patients has re-opened pursuant to sub-paragraph (9)(a), it will nevertheless close again if, during the period specified by the assessment panel as the period for which the list should remain closed, the number of the contractor's registered patients rise to the number specified by the assessment panel in accordance with sub-paragraph (7)(b) as the number of registered patients which, if that number were reached, would trigger the re-closure of the contractor's list of patients.

(11) Except in cases where the contractor's list of patients is already open pursuant to sub-paragraph (9), the Health Board must notify the contractor in writing between 7 and 14 days before the expiry of the closure period specified in sub-paragraph (8), confirming the date on which the contractor's list of patients will re-open.

(12) Where the assessment panel rejects the list closure in accordance with sub-paragraph (6)(b), that list must remain open, and the Health Board and the contractor must enter into discussions with a view to ensuring that the contractor receives support from the Health Board which will enable the contractor to continue to provide services safely and effectively.

(13) An assessment panel which rejects the list closure in accordance with sub-paragraph (6)(b) must specify the number of registered patients (expressed either in absolute terms or as a percentage of the number of such patients specified as the current number of the contractor's registered patients), which if that number were reached, would trigger the closure of the contractor's list of patients.

(14) Where a list closure is triggered in accordance with sub-paragraph (13), a contractor must notify the Health Board to confirm the date the list closure was triggered and the details specified in paragraph 26(9).

(15) Where the assessment panel rejects the list closure in accordance with sub-paragraph (6)(b), the contractor may not submit a further closure notice as described in paragraph 26 until—

- (a) the expiry of a period of six months beginning with the date of the assessment panel's determination; or
- (b) (if applicable) the final determination of the NHS dispute resolution procedure (or any court proceedings),

whichever is the later unless there has been a change in the circumstances of the contractor which affects its ability to deliver services under the contract.

(16) Any decision or determination by the assessment panel for the purposes of this paragraph may be reached by a majority.

Assignment of patients to lists: open lists

29.—(1) A Health Board may, subject to paragraph 31, assign a new patient to a contractor whose list of patients is open.

(2) In this paragraph and in paragraphs 30 and 32 to 34, a "new" patient means a person who—

- (a) is resident (whether or not temporarily) within the area of the Health Board;
- (b) has been refused inclusion in a list of patients of, or has not been accepted as a temporary resident by, a contractor whose premises are within such an area; and
- (c) wishes to be included in the list of patients of a contractor whose practice premises are within that area.

Assignment of patients to lists: closed lists

30.—(1) A Health Board may not assign a new patient to a contractor which has closed its list of patients except in the circumstances specified in sub-paragraph (2).

(2) A Health Board may, subject to paragraph 31, assign a new patient to a contractor whose practice premises are within the Health Board's area and which has closed its list of patients, if—

(a) most or all of the providers of essential services (or their equivalent) whose practice premises are within the Health Board's area have closed their lists of patients;

(b) the assessment panel has determined under paragraph 32(7) that patients may be assigned to the contractor in question, and that determination has not been overturned either by a determination of the Scottish Ministers or the adjudicator under the NHS dispute resolution procedure as modified by paragraph 33(3) or (where applicable) by a court; and

(c) the Health Board has entered into discussions with the contractor in question regarding the assignment of a patient if such discussions are required under paragraph 34.

Factors relevant to assignments

31. In making an assignment to a contractor under paragraph 29 or 30, the Health Board is to have regard to—

(a) the wishes and circumstances of the patient to be assigned;

(b) the distance between the patient's place of residence and the contractor's practice premises;

(c) whether, during the six months ending on the date on which the application for assignment is received by the Health Board, the patient's name has been removed from the list of patients of any contractor in the area of the Health Board under paragraph 17 or its equivalent provision in relation to a section 17C provider in the area of the Health Board;

(d) whether the patient's name has been removed from the list of patients of any contractor in the area of the Health Board under paragraph 18 or its equivalent provision in relation to a section 17C provider in the area of the Health Board and, if so, whether the contractor has appropriate facilities to deal with such a patient; and

(e) such other matters as the Health Board considers to be relevant.

Assignments to closed lists: determinations of the assessment panel

32.—(1) This paragraph applies where most or all of the providers of essential services (or their equivalent) whose practice premises are within the area of a Health Board have closed their lists of patients.

(2) If the Health Board wishes to assign new patients to contractors which have closed their lists of patients, it must prepare a proposal to be considered by the assessment panel, and the proposal must include details of those contractors to which the Health Board wishes to assign patients.

(3) The Health Board must ensure that an assessment panel is appointed by another Health Board to consider and determine its proposal made under sub-paragraph (2).

(4) The Health Board must notify in writing—

(a) contractors or section 17C providers whose practice premises are within the Health Board's area which—

  (i) have closed their list of patients; and

  (ii) may, in the opinion of the Health Board, be affected by the determination of the assessment panel; and

(b) the area medical committee (if any) for the area of the Health Board,

that it has referred the matter to the assessment panel.

(5) In reaching its determination, the assessment panel must have regard to relevant factors including—

(a) whether the Health Board has attempted to secure the provision of essential services (or their equivalent) for new patients other than by means of their assignment to contractors with closed lists of patients; and

(b) the workload of those contractors likely to be affected by any decision to assign such patients to their list of patients.

(6) The assessment panel must reach a determination within the period of 28 days beginning with the date on which the panel was appointed.

(7) The assessment panel must determine whether the Health Board may assign patients to contractors which have closed their lists of patients; and if it determines that the Health Board may make such assignments, it must also determine those contractors to which patients may be assigned.

(8) The assessment panel may determine that the Health Board may assign patients to contractors other than those contractors specified by the Health Board in its proposal under sub-paragraph (2), as long as the contractors were notified under sub-paragraph (4)(a).

(9) The assessment panel's determination must include its comments on the matters specified in sub-paragraph (5), and must be notified in writing to those contractors which were notified under sub-paragraph (4)(a).

(10) Any decision or determination by the assessment panel for the purposes of this paragraph may be reached by a majority.

Assignments to closed lists: NHS dispute resolution procedure relating to determinations of the assessment panel

33.—(1) Where an assessment panel makes a determination under paragraph 32(7) that the Health Board may assign new patients to contractors which have closed their lists of patients, any contractor specified in that determination may refer the matter to the Scottish Ministers to review the determination of the assessment panel.

(2) Where more than one contractor specified in the determination in accordance with paragraph 32(7) wishes to refer the matter for dispute resolution, those contractors may, if they all agree, refer the matter jointly, and in that case the Scottish Ministers must review the matter in relation to those contractors together.

(3) Where a matter is referred to the Scottish Ministers under sub-paragraph (1) or (2), it will be determined in accordance with the NHS dispute resolution procedure as modified as follows—

(a) in paragraph 91(3), for "a dispute as mentioned in sub-paragraph (1)" substitute "the matter as mentioned in paragraph 33(1)";

(b) for paragraph 91(4) substitute—

"(4) The contractor (or contractors) wishing to refer the matter as mentioned in paragraph 33(1) or (2) must send the request to the Scottish Ministers within the period of 7 days beginning with the date of the determination by the assessment panel in accordance with paragraph 32(7).";

(c) for paragraph 91(13) substitute—

"(13) In this paragraph, "specified period" means such period as the Scottish Ministers specify in the request sent under sub-paragraphs (6) or (8), being not less than one, nor more than two, weeks beginning with the date on which the request is given, but the adjudicator may, if the period for determination of the dispute has been extended in accordance with sub-paragraph (19), extend any such period (even after it has expired) and, where the adjudicator does so, a reference in this paragraph to the specified period is to the period as so extended.";

(d) after paragraph 91(15), insert—

"(16) Subject to sub-paragraph (19), within the period of 21 days beginning with the date on which the matter was referred to the Scottish Ministers, the adjudicator must determine whether the Health Board may assign patients to contractors which have closed their lists of patients; and if the adjudicator determines that the Health Board may make such assignments, the adjudicator must also determine those contractors to which patients may be assigned.

(17) The adjudicator may not determine that patients may be assigned to a contractor which was not specified in the determination of the assessment panel under paragraph 32(7).

(18) In the case of a matter referred jointly by contractors in accordance with paragraph 33(2), the adjudicator may determine that patients may be assigned to one, some or all of the contractors which referred the matter.

(19) The period of 21 days referred to in sub-paragraph (16) may be extended (even after it has expired) by a further specified number of days if an agreement to that effect is reached by—

(a) the adjudicator;

(b) the Health Board"; and

(e) the contractor (or contractors) which referred the matter to dispute resolution." and;(e)paragraph 92(2) does not apply.

Assignments to closed lists: assignments of patients by a Health Board

34.—(1) Before the Health Board may assign a new patient to a contractor, it must, subject to sub-paragraph (3), enter into discussions with that contractor regarding additional support that the Health Board can offer the contractor, and the Health Board must use its best endeavours to provide appropriate support.

(2) In the discussions referred to in sub-paragraph (1), both parties must use reasonable endeavours to reach agreement.

(3) The requirement in sub-paragraph (1) to enter into discussions applies—

(a) to the first assignment of a patient to a particular contractor; and

(b) to any subsequent assignment to that contractor to the extent that it is reasonable and appropriate having regard to the numbers of patients who have been or may be assigned to it and the period of time since the last discussions under sub-paragraph (1) took place.

Assignments of patients to lists at request of contractor

35.—(1) A Health Board may, subject to sub-paragraph (3), at the request of a contractor, assign a patient on that contractor's list of patients to a receiving contractor's list of patients.

(2) A request under sub-paragraph (1) must be notified in writing to the Health Board and confirm that—

(a) the patient has given written consent to the assignment; and

(b) the requesting and receiving contractors have agreed to the assignment.

(3) An assignment under this paragraph may only be made where either the requesting contractor or receiving contractor have varied their practice area in accordance with paragraph 36.

(4) In this paragraph, "a receiving contractor" may include a contractor who has closed its list of patients.

Application for variation of a practice area

36.—(1) A contractor may request a variation of their practice area by notifying the Health Board in writing of its variation request.

(2) The Health Board must—

(a) enter into discussions with the contractor regarding the variation request mentioned in sub-paragraph (1) within a period of 1 month beginning with the date of receipt of the notification referred to in that sub-paragraph; and

(b) have concluded such discussions within a period of 3 months beginning with the date of the receipt of the notification mentioned in sub-paragraph (1).

(3) Following the discussions mentioned in sub-paragraph (2), the Health Board must—

(a) consult with the Area Medical Committee regarding the contractor's variation request;

(b) consider the effect of the variation request mentioned in sub-paragraph (1) on the practice areas of other contractors within its Health Board area; and

(c) taking account of the discussions mentioned in sub-paragraph (2) and the factors at sub-head (a) and (b), approve or reject the contractor's variation request.

(4) The Health Board must notify the contractor in writing as soon as possible of its decision to approve or reject the variation request in accordance with sub-paragraph (3).

(5) A notification of approval mentioned in sub-paragraph (4) must confirm the date the variation is to take effect.

Rejection of a practice area variation request

37.—(1) This paragraph applies where the Health Board rejects the variation request in accordance with paragraph 36(3).

(2) The contractor and the Health Board may not refer the matter for determination in accordance with the NHS dispute resolution procedure (or, where applicable, commence court proceedings) until the assessment panel has given its determination in accordance with the following sub-paragraphs.

(3) The Health Board must ensure that an assessment panel is appointed by another Health Board as soon as is practicable to consider and determine whether the contractor should be permitted to vary its practice area.

(4) The Health Board must provide the assessment panel with such information as the assessment panel may reasonably require to enable the panel to reach a determination and must include in such information any written observations received from the contractor.

(5) Within a period of three months beginning with the date on which the Health Board rejected the variation request, the assessment panel must—

(a) approve the variation request; or

(b) reject the variation request,

and must notify the Health Board and the contractor of its determination in writing as soon as possible.

(6) Where the assessment panel approves a variation request in accordance with sub-paragraph (5)(a), it must specify the date from which the variation of the practice area takes effect.

(7) Where the assessment panel rejects the variation request in accordance with sub-paragraph (5)(b), the contractor may not request a further practice area variation under paragraph 36 until whichever is the later of the following dates—

(a) the expiry of a period of one year beginning with the date of the assessment panel's determination; or

(b) (if applicable) the final determination of the NHS dispute resolution procedure (or any court proceedings).

(8) Any decision or determination by the assessment panel for the purposes of this paragraph may be reached by a majority.

PART 3

PRESCRIBING AND DISPENSING

Prescribing

38. The contractor is to ensure that any prescription form for drugs, medicines or appliances issued or created by a prescriber complies as appropriate with the requirements in paragraphs 39 to 41.

Prescribing

39.—(1) Subject to paragraphs 40 and 41 a prescriber is to order any drugs, medicines or appliances which are needed for the treatment of any patient who is receiving treatment under the contract by—

(a) issuing to that patient a non-electronic prescription form; or

(b) creating and transmitting an electronic prescription form,

and such a non-electronic prescription form or electronic prescription form must not be used in any other circumstances.

(2) In issuing any non-electronic prescription form, the prescriber must sign the prescription form in ink with the prescriber's initials, or forenames, and surname in the prescriber's own handwriting and not by means of a stamp and must so sign only after particulars of the order have been inserted in the prescription form.

(3) A prescription form must not refer to any previous prescription form.

(4) A separate prescription form must be used for each patient.

(5) In a case of urgency a prescriber may request a pharmacist to dispense a drug or medicine before a prescription form is issued or created, only if —

(a) that drug or medicine is not a Scheduled drug;

(b) that drug is not a controlled drug within the meaning of the Misuse of Drugs Act 1971(**a**) other than a drug which is for the time being specified in schedules 4 or 5 of the Misuse of Drugs Regulations 2001(**b**); and

(c) the prescriber undertakes to furnish the pharmacist, within 72 hours, with a prescription form completed in accordance with sub-paragraph (2) or with an electronic prescription form.

(6) In a case of urgency a prescriber may request a pharmacist to dispense an appliance before a prescription form is issued or created only if—

(a) that appliance does not contain a Scheduled drug or a controlled drug within the meaning of the Misuse of Drugs Act 1971, other than a drug which is for the time being specified in schedule 5 of the Misuse of Drugs Regulations 2001;

(b) in the case of a restricted availability appliance, the patient is a person, or it is for a purpose specified in the Drug Tariff; and

(c) the prescriber undertakes to furnish the pharmacist, within 72 hours, with a prescription form completed in accordance with sub-paragraph (2) or with an electronic prescription form.

(7) A prescriber may only order drugs, medicines or appliances by means of an electronic prescription form if the prescription is not for a controlled drug within the meaning of the Misuse

---

(**a**) 1971 c.38. Section 2 was relevantly amended by paragraph 2 of schedule 17 of the Police Reform and Social Responsibility Act 2011 (c.13).
(**b**) S.I. 2001/3998. Schedule 4 was amended by S.I. 2009/3136, S.I. 2013/625, S.I. 2014/3277, S.I. 2015/891 and S.I. 2016/1125. Schedule 5 was amended by S.I. 2005/2864.

of Drugs Act 1971, other than a drug which is for the time being specified in schedule 4 or 5 of the Misuse of Drugs Regulations 2001.

(8) A prescriber who orders drugs, medicines or appliances by means of an electronic prescription form must issue the patient with a written record of the prescription which has been created.

Restrictions on prescribing by medical practitioners

40.—(1) In the course of treating a patient to whom a medical practitioner is providing treatment under the contract, the medical practitioner must not order on a prescription form a drug, medicine or other substance specified in any directions given by the Scottish Ministers under section 17N(6) of the Act (Other mandatory contract terms)(**a**) as being drugs, medicines or other substances which may not be ordered for patients in the provision of medical services under the contract but may, subject to regulation 28(2)(b), prescribe such a drug or other substance for that patient in the course of that treatment under a private arrangement.

(2) In the course of treating a patient to whom a medical practitioner is providing treatment under the contract, the medical practitioner must not order on a prescription form a drug, medicine or other substance specified in any directions given by the Scottish Ministers under section 17N(6) of the Act as being a drug, medicine or other substance which can only be ordered for specified patients and specified purposes unless—

   (a) that patient is a person of the specified description;

   (b) that drug, medicine or other substance is prescribed for that patient only for the specified purpose; and

   (c) the practitioner includes on the prescription form the reference "SLS",

but may, subject to regulation 28(2)(b), prescribe such a drug, medicine or other substance for that patient in the course of that treatment under a private arrangement.

(3) In the course of treating a patient to whom a medical practitioner is providing treatment under the contract, the medical practitioner must not order on a prescription form a restricted availability appliance unless—

   (a) the patient is a person, or it is for a purpose, specified in the Drug Tariff; and

   (b) the practitioner includes on the prescription form the reference "SLS",

but may, subject to regulation 28(2)(b), prescribe such an appliance for that patient in the course of that treatment under a private arrangement.

Restrictions on prescribing by supplementary prescribers

41.—(1) The contractor must have arrangements in place to secure that a supplementary prescriber will—

   (a) issue or create a prescription for a prescription only medicine;

   (b) administer a prescription only medicine for parenteral administration; or

   (c) give directions for the administration of a prescription only medicine for parenteral administration,

as a supplementary prescriber, under the conditions set out in sub-paragraph (2).

(2) The conditions referred to in sub-paragraph (1) are that—

   (a) the supplementary prescriber satisfies the applicable conditions set out in regulation 215 of the Human Medicines Regulations 2012 (prescribing and administration by supplementary prescribers)(**b**), unless those conditions do not apply by virtue of any of the exemptions set out in the subsequent provisions of those Regulations;

(**a**) Section 17N was inserted by section 4 of the Primary Medical Services (Scotland) Act 2004 (asp 1).
(**b**) S.I. 2012/1916.

(b) the drug, medicine or other substance is not specified in any directions given by the Scottish Ministers under section 17N(6) of the Act as being a drug, medicine or other substance which may not be ordered for patients in the provision of medical services under the contract;

(c) the drug, medicine or other substance is not specified in any directions given by the Scottish Ministers under section 17N(6) of the Act as being a drug, medicine or other substance which can only be ordered for specified patients and specified purposes unless—

   (i) the patient is a person of the specified description;

   (ii) the medicine is prescribed for that patient only for the specified purposes; and

   (iii) if the supplementary prescriber is issuing or creating the prescription form, the supplementary prescriber includes on the prescription form the reference "SLS".

(3) Where the functions of a supplementary prescriber include prescribing, the contractor must have arrangements in place to secure that that person will only issue or create a prescription for—

(a) an appliance; or

(b) a medicine which is not a prescription only medicine,

as a supplementary prescriber under the conditions set out in sub-paragraph (4).

(4) The conditions referred to in sub-paragraph (3) are that—

(a) the supplementary prescriber acts in accordance with a clinical management plan which is in effect at the time the supplementary prescriber acts and which contains the following particulars—

   (i) the name of the patient to whom the plan relates;

   (ii) the illness or conditions which may be treated by the supplementary prescriber;

   (iii) the date on which the plan is to take effect, and when it is to be reviewed by the medical practitioner or dentist who is a party to the plan;

   (iv) reference to the class or description of medicines or types of appliances which may be prescribed or administered under the plan;

   (v) any restrictions or limitations as to the strength or dose of any medicine which may be prescribed or administered under the plan, and any period of administration or use of any medicine or appliance which may be prescribed or administered under the plan;

   (vi) relevant warnings about known sensitivities of the patient to, or known difficulties of the patient with, particular medicines or appliances;

   (vii) the arrangements for notification of—

      (aa) suspected or known adverse reactions to any medicine which may be prescribed or administered under the plan, and suspected or known adverse reactions to any other medicine taken at the same time as any medicine prescribed or administered under the plan;

      (bb) incidents occurring with the appliance which might lead, might have led or has led to the death or serious deterioration of state of the health of the patient, and

   (viii) the circumstances in which the supplementary prescriber should refer to, or seek the advice of, the medical practitioner or dentist who is a party to the plan;

(b) the supplementary prescriber has access to the health records of the patient to whom the plan relates which are used by any medical practitioner or dentist who is a party to the plan;

(c) if it is a prescription for a drug, medicine or other substance, that drug, medicine or other substance is not specified in any directions given by the Scottish Ministers under section 17N(6) of the Act as being a drug, medicine or other substance which may not be ordered for patients in the provision of primary medical services under a general medical services contract;

(d) if it is a prescription for an appliance, the appliance is listed in Parts 2 to 6 or 8 to 10 of the Drug Tariff; and

(e) if it is a prescription for a restricted availability appliance—

  (i) the patient is a person of a description mentioned in the entry in Part 3 of the Drug Tariff in respect of that appliance;

  (ii) the appliance is prescribed only for the purposes specified in respect of that person in that entry; and

  (iii) when issuing or creating the prescription form, the supplementary prescriber includes on the prescription form the reference "SLS".

(5) In sub-paragraph (4)(a), "clinical management plan" means a plan (which may be amended from time to time) relating to the treatment of an individual patient agreed by—

(a) the patient to whom the plan relates;

(b) the medical practitioner or dentist who is a party to the plan; and

(c) any supplementary prescriber who is to prescribe, give directions for administration or administer under the plan.

Interpretation of paragraphs 38 to 41

42. For the purposes of paragraphs 38 to 41, in their application to a contractor whose contract includes the provision of contraceptive services, drugs includes contraceptive substances and appliances includes contraceptive appliances.

Excessive prescribing

43.—(1) The contractor must not prescribe drugs, medicines or appliances whose cost or quantity, in relation to any patient, is, by reason of the character of the drug, medicine or appliance in question in excess of that which was reasonably necessary for the proper treatment of that patient.

(2) In considering whether a contractor has breached its obligations under sub-paragraph (1), the Health Board must seek the views of the area medical committee for its area.

Provision of dispensing services

44.—(1) A contractor may secure the provision of dispensing services to its registered patients only if it is authorised or required to do so by the Health Board in accordance with this paragraph.

(2) Where the Health Board, is satisfied, after consultation with the area pharmaceutical committee, that a person, by reason of—

(a) distance;

(b) inadequacy of means of communication; or

(c) other exceptional circumstances,

will have serious difficulty in obtaining from a pharmacist any drugs, medicines or appliances, other than Scheduled drugs, required for that person's treatment, the Health Board may require or authorise the contractor with whom the person is a registered patient to supply such drugs, medicines and appliances to that person until further notice.

(3) Notwithstanding anything contained in sub-paragraph (2)—

(a) a contractor will not be required to undertake the supply of drugs, medicines, and appliances under sub-paragraph (2) if the contractor satisfies the Health Board that the contractor is not in the habit of dispensing drugs, medicines, and appliances for the contractor's patients;

(b) a contractor must receive reasonable notice from the Health Board that the contractor is required to undertake the supply of drugs, medicines and appliances under sub-paragraph (2) or that such supply is to be discontinued.

(4) A contractor must receive the support of an appropriately qualified pharmacist independent prescriber provided by the Health Board, where the Health Board considers that the health outcomes of patients are likely to be improved by the contractor and pharmacist independent prescriber working together with the aim of ensuring that the patient gets the best clinical benefit from their prescribed medicines.

(5) Subject to sub-paragraph (7), a contractor, who is required by the Health Board to supply drugs, medicines and appliances under sub-paragraph (2) to a patient, in the course of treating that patient under these Regulations—

(a) must, subject to sub-paragraph (7), record on a prescription form completed in accordance with paragraph 39, an order for supply of any drugs, medicines or appliances which are needed for the treatment of that patient, but is not required to issue that form to that patient;

(b) is to supply those drugs, medicines or appliances for that patient under sub-paragraph (2) but—

(i) must not supply under sub-paragraph (2) for that patient any Scheduled drug specified as being a drug, medicine or other substance which may not be ordered for patients in the provision of medical services under the contract, except that, where the contractor has ordered a drug which has an appropriate non-proprietary name either by that name or by its formula, the contractor may supply a drug which has the same specification notwithstanding that it is such a Scheduled drug (but, in the case of a drug which combines more than one drug, only if the combination has an appropriate non-proprietary name);

(ii) will supply under sub-paragraph (2) for that patient any Scheduled drug specified as being a drug, medicine or other substance which may only be ordered for specific patients and purposes only where—

(aa) that patient is a person of the specified description; and

(bb) that drug, medicine or other substance is supplied to that patient only for the specified purpose;

(iii) will supply under sub-paragraph (2) for that patient a restricted availability appliance only if it is for a patient in a category of person or a purpose specified in the Drug Tariff;

(c) may supply for that patient with the contractor's consent, in respect of that treatment but otherwise than under sub-paragraph (2), any Scheduled drug.

(6) A contractor must comply with any arrangements made by the Scottish Ministers, or made by the Health Board after consultation with the area medical committee (if any) and the area pharmaceutical committee and approved by the Scottish Ministers, under which the contractor may obtain and have available any drugs, medicines or appliances which the contractor is required or entitled to supply in terms of this paragraph.

(7) Sub-paragraph (5) does not apply to drugs, medicines or appliances ordered on a prescription form by a supplementary prescriber, or an independent prescriber.

(8) Where a patient presents an order on a non-electronic prescription form for listed drugs or medicines, or appliances, signed by a supplementary prescriber, or an independent prescriber, to a contractor who is required under sub-paragraph (2) to provide drugs or appliances to that patient or a contractor who is required under sub-paragraph (2) to provide drugs or appliances to a patient receives from the ePharmacy service an electronic prescription form which contains an order for listed drugs or medicines, or appliances in respect of that patient, signed by a supplementary prescriber, or an independent prescriber, the contractor may provide to the patient such drugs, medicines or appliances so ordered as the contractor supplies in the normal course of the contractor's practice.

(9) A drug supplied by a contractor unless administered in person must be supplied in a suitable container.

(10) Nothing in this paragraph prevents a contractor providing a Scheduled drug or a restricted availability appliance in the course of treating a patient under a private arrangement.

Provision of drugs, medicines and appliances for immediate treatment or personal administration

45.—(1) Subject to sub-paragraph (2), a contractor—

(a) is to provide to a patient any drug, medicine or appliance, not being a Scheduled drug, where such provision is needed for the immediate treatment of that patient before provision can otherwise be obtained; and

(b) may provide to a patient any drug, medicine or appliance, not being a Scheduled drug, which the contractor personally administers or applies to that patient,

but may, in either case, provide a restricted availability appliance only if it is for a person or a purpose specified in the Drug Tariff.

(2) Nothing in sub-paragraph (1) authorises a person to supply any drug or medicine to a patient otherwise than in accordance with Part 3 of the Medicines Act 1968(**a**) or any regulations or orders made thereunder.

PART 4

PERSONS WHO PERFORM SERVICES

Qualifications of performers

46.—(1) Subject to sub-paragraph (2), no medical practitioner may perform medical services under the contract unless the practitioner is—

(a) included in the primary medical services performers' list for the Health Board which is under a duty to provide or secure the provision of the service to be performed;

(b) not suspended from that list or from the Medical Register; and

(c) not subject to interim suspension under section 41A of the Medical Act 1983 (interim orders)(**b**).

(2) Sub-paragraph (1)(a) does not apply in the case of—

(a) a medical practitioner employed in Scotland, by a Health Board, in England and Wales, by an NHS trust, an NHS foundation trust, or, in Northern Ireland, by a Health and Social Care trust who is providing services other than primary medical services at the practice premises;

(b) a person who is provisionally registered under section 15 (provisional registration), 15A (provisional registration for EEA nationals) or 21 (provisional registration of EEA nationals with certain overseas qualifications) of the Medical Act 1983(**c**) acting in the course of the person's employment in a resident medical capacity in an approved practice setting within the meaning of section 44D of the Medical Act 1983 (approved practice settings)(**d**); or

---

(**a**) 1968 c.67. Part 3 was amended by S.I. 1984/187, section 1 of the Medical Products: Prescription by Nurses etc. Act 1992 (c.28), S.I. 1993/2538, S.I. 1994/105, S.I. 1994/3142 S.I. 1994/3144, S.I. 1997/322, S.I. 1998/108, section 63 of the Health and Care Social Care Act 2001 (c.5), S.I. 2002/236 S.I. 2002/253, S.I. 2003/1590, S.I. 2004/1771, S.I. 2005/2789, S.I. 2006/1916, S.I. 2006/2407, section 220(c) of the Health and Social Care Act 2012 (c.7) and S.I. 2012/1916.
(**b**) 1983 c.54. Section 41A was inserted by S.I. 2000/1803 and amended by S.I. 2002/3135, S.I. 2006/1914 and S.I. 2015/794.
(**c**) Section 15 was substituted by S.I. 2006/1914. Section 15A was inserted by S.I. 2000/3041 and amended by S.I. 2006/1914, S.I. 2007/3101 and S.I. 2011/1043. Section 21 was amended by S.I. 2002/3135, S.I. 2006/1914 and S.I. 2007/3101.
(**d**) Section 44D was inserted by S.I. 2006/1914.

(c) a GP Registrar who has applied to the Health Board to have the GP Registrar's name included in the primary medical services performers list of the Health Board, until the first of the following events arises—

  (i) the Health Board notifies the GP Registrar of the Board's decision on that application;

  (ii) the end of a period of 2 months, starting with the date on which the GP Registrar's vocational training scheme begins.

(3) In this paragraph, "vocational training scheme" has the meaning given in regulation 2 (interpretation) of the National Health Service (Primary Medical Services Performers Lists) (Scotland) Regulations 2004(**a**).

Qualifications of performers

47. No health care professional other than one to whom paragraph 46 applies may perform clinical services under the contract unless the health care professional is appropriately registered with the health care professional's relevant professional body and the health care professional's registration is not currently suspended.

Qualifications of performers

48. Where the registration of a health care professional or, in the case of a medical practitioner, the practitioner's inclusion in a list, is subject to conditions, the contractor must ensure compliance with those conditions insofar as they are relevant to the contract.

Qualifications of performers

49. No health care professional may perform any clinical services unless the health care professional has such clinical experience and training as are necessary to enable the health care professional properly to perform such services.

Conditions for employment and engagement

50.—(1) Subject to sub-paragraphs (2) and (3), a contractor must not employ or engage a medical practitioner (other than one falling within paragraph 46(2)) unless—

(a) that practitioner has provided it with the name and address of the Health Board on whose primary medical services performers list the practitioner appears; and

(b) the contractor has checked that the practitioner meets the requirements in paragraph 46.

(2) Where the employment or engagement of a medical practitioner is urgently needed and it is not possible for the contractor to check the matters referred to in paragraph 46 in accordance with sub-paragraph (1)(b) before employing or engaging the practitioner, the practitioner may be employed or engaged on a temporary basis for a single period of up to 7 days whilst such checks are undertaken.

(3) Where the prospective employee is a GP Registrar, the requirements set out in sub-paragraph (1) apply with the modifications that—

(a) the name and address provided under sub-paragraph (1) may be the name and address of the Health Board on whose primary medical services performers list the GP Registrar has applied for inclusion; and

(b) confirmation that the GP Registrar's name appears on that list will not be required until the end of the first two months of the GP Registrar's training period.

(**a**) S.S.I. 2004/114 was relevantly amended by S.I. 2010/234.

Conditions for employment and engagement

51.—(1) A contractor must not employ or engage—

(a) a health care professional (other than one to whom paragraph 46 applies) unless the contractor has checked that the health care professional meets the requirements in paragraph 47; or

(b) a health care professional to perform clinical services unless the contractor has taken reasonable steps to satisfy itself that the health care professional meets the requirements in paragraph 49.

(2) Where the employment or engagement of a health care professional is urgently needed and it is not possible to check the matters referred to in paragraph 47 in accordance with sub-paragraph (1) before employing or engaging that person, the health care professional may be employed or engaged on a temporary basis for a single period of up to 7 days whilst such checks are undertaken.

(3) When considering a health care professional's experience and training for the purposes of sub-paragraph (1)(b), the contractor must have regard in particular to—

(a) any post-graduate or post-registration qualification held by the health care professional; and

(b) any relevant training undertaken by the health care professional and any relevant clinical experience gained by the health care professional.

Conditions for employment and engagement

52.—(1) The contractor must not employ or engage a health care professional to perform medical services under the contract unless—

(a) that person has provided two clinical references, relating to two recent posts (which may include any current post) as a health care professional which lasted for three months without a significant break, or where this is not possible, a full explanation and alternative referees; and

(b) the contractor has checked and is satisfied with the references.

(2) Where the employment or engagement of a medical practitioner is urgently needed and it is not possible to obtain and check the references in accordance with sub-paragraph (1)(b) before employing or engaging the practitioner, the practitioner may be employed or engaged on a temporary basis for a single period of up to 14 days whilst the practitioner's references are checked and considered, and for an additional single period of a further 7 days if the contractor believes the person supplying those references is ill, on holiday or otherwise temporarily unavailable.

(3) Where the contractor employs or engages the same person on more than one occasion within a period of three months, it may rely on the references provided on the first occasion, provided that those references are not more than twelve months old.

Conditions for employment and engagement

53.—(1) Before employing or engaging any person to assist it in the provision of services under the contract, the contractor must take reasonable care to satisfy itself that the person in question is both suitably qualified and competent to discharge the duties for which the person is to be employed or engaged.

(2) The duty imposed by sub-paragraph (1) is in addition to the duties imposed by paragraphs 50 to 52.

(3) When considering the competence and suitability of any person for the purpose of sub-paragraph (1), the contractor must have regard, in particular, to—

(a) that person's academic and vocational qualifications;

(b) that person's education and training; and

(c) that person's previous employment or work experience.

Training

54. The contractor must ensure that for any health care professional who is—

(a) performing clinical services under the contract; or

(b) employed or engaged to assist in the performance of such services,

there are in place arrangements for the purpose of maintaining and updating the health care professional's skills and knowledge in relation to the services which the health care professional is performing or assisting in performing.

Training

55. The contractor must afford to each employee reasonable opportunities to undertake appropriate training with a view to maintaining that employee's competence.

Terms and conditions

56. The contractor may only offer employment to a general medical practitioner on terms and conditions which are no less favourable than those contained in the "Model terms and conditions of service for a salaried general practitioner employed by a GMS practice" published by the British Medical Association and the NHS Confederation as item 1.2 of the supplementary documents to the GMS contract 2003(**a**).

Arrangements for GP Registrars

57.—(1) The contractor may only employ or engage a GP Registrar subject to the conditions in sub-paragraph (2).

(2) The conditions referred to in sub-paragraph (1) are that the contractor must not, by reason only of having employed or engaged a GP Registrar, reduce the total number of hours for which other medical practitioners perform primary medical services under the contract or for which other staff assist them in the performance of those services.

(3) A contractor which employs or engages a GP Registrar is to—

(a) offer the GP Registrar terms of employment in accordance with the rates and subject to the conditions contained in any directions given by the Scottish Ministers to NHS Education for Scotland(**b**) concerning the grants, fees, travelling and other allowances payable to GP Registrars; and

(b) take into account any guidance issued by the Scottish Ministers in relation to the GP Registrar Scheme(**c**).

Independent prescribers and supplementary prescribers

58.—(1) Where—

(a) a contractor employs or engages a person who is an independent prescriber or a supplementary prescriber whose functions will include prescribing;

(**a**) This document is published jointly by the General Practitioners Committee of the British Medical Association and the NHS Confederation.
(**b**) NHS Education Scotland is a Special Health Board established under section 2(1)(b) of the Act by S.S.I. 2002/103 (as relevantly amended by S.S.I. 2006/79) which applies section 2(5) of the Act to NHS Education Scotland as it applies to Health Boards.
(**c**) The current guidance is PCS(GPR) 2009/1, which is available at http://www.sehd.scot.nhs.uk/pcs/PCS2009(GPR)01.pdf, as amended by PCS(GPR) 2011/1, which is available at http://www.sehd.scot.nhs.uk/pcs/PCS2011(GPR)01.pdf and as amended by PCS(GPR) 2015/1, which is available at http://www.sehd.scot.nhs.uk/pcs/PCS2015(GPR)01.pdf.

(b) a contractor is a partnership or limited liability partnership and one of the partners or members as the case may be is an independent prescriber or a supplementary prescriber whose functions will include prescribing;

(c) a contractor is a company and one of the members is an independent prescriber or a supplementary prescriber whose functions will include prescribing; or

(d) the functions of a person who is an independent prescriber or a supplementary prescriber whom the contractor already employs or has already engaged are extended to include prescribing,

it must notify the Health Board in writing within the period of 7 days beginning with the date on which the contractor employed or engaged the person, the person became a partner or member as the case may be of the partnership, limited liability partnership or company that is a party to the contract (unless, immediately before becoming such a partner or member of that partnership, limited liability partnership or company that is such a party, the person fell under sub-paragraph (1)(a)) or the person's functions were extended as the case may be.

(2) Where—

(a) the contractor ceases to employ or engage a person who is an independent prescriber or a supplementary prescriber whose functions included prescribing;

(b) the partner or member, as the case may be, in a partnership or limited liability partnership who is an independent prescriber or a supplementary prescriber whose functions include prescribing, ceases to be a partner or member of the partnership or limited liability partnership;

(c) the member of a company who is an independent prescriber or a supplementary prescriber whose functions include prescribing, ceases to be a member of the company;

(d) the functions of a person who is an independent prescriber or a supplementary prescriber whom the contractor employs or engages in its practice are changed so that they no longer include prescribing; or

(e) the contractor becomes aware that a person who is an independent prescriber or a supplementary prescriber whom the contractor employs or engages has been removed or suspended from the relevant register,

it must notify the Health Board in writing by the end of the second working day after the day when the event occurred.

(3) The contractor must provide the following information when it notifies the Health Board in accordance with sub-paragraph (1)—

(a) the person's full name;

(b) the person's professional qualifications;

(c) the person's identifying number which appears in the relevant register;

(d) the date on which the person's entry in the relevant register was annotated to the effect that the person was qualified to order drugs, medicines and appliances for patients;

(e) the date on which—

(i) the person was employed or engaged, if applicable;

(ii) the person became a partner or member, as the case may be in the partnership or limited liability partnership, if applicable;

(iii) the person became a member of the company, if applicable; or

(iv) one of the person's functions became prescribing in its practice.

(4) The contractor must provide the following information when it notifies the Health Board in accordance with sub-paragraph (2)—

(a) the person's full name;

(b) the person's professional qualifications;

(c) the person's identifying number which appears in the relevant register;

(d) the date on which—
- (i) the person ceased to be employed or engaged in its practice;
- (ii) the person ceased to be a partner or member, as the case may be in the partnership or limited liability partnership;
- (iii) the person ceased to be a member of the company;
- (iv) the person's functions changed so as no longer to include prescribing; or
- (v) the person was removed or suspended from the relevant register.

Signing of documents

59.—(1) In addition to any other requirements relating to such documents whether in these Regulations or otherwise, the contractor must ensure that the documents specified in sub-paragraph (2) include—

(a) the clinical profession of the health care professional who signed the document; and

(b) the name of the contractor on whose behalf it is signed.

(2) The documents referred to in sub-paragraph (1) are—

(a) certificates issued in accordance with regulation 25, unless regulations relating to particular certificates provide otherwise;

(b) prescription forms; and

(c) any other clinical documents.

Level of skill

60. The contractor must carry out its obligations under the contract with reasonable skill and care.

Appraisal and assessment

61.—(1) The contractor must ensure that any medical practitioner performing services under the contract—

(a) participates in the appraisal system provided by the Health Board unless the practitioner participates in an appropriate appraisal system provided by another health service body or is an armed forces GP; and

(b) co-operates with any assessment process which the Health Board operates in relation to poorly performing doctors, as set out in NHS circular PCA(M)(2001)17(**a**).

(2) The Health Board must provide an appraisal system for the purposes of sub-paragraph (1)(a) after consultation with the area medical committee and such other persons as appear to the Health Board to be appropriate.

(3) In sub-paragraph (1)—

"armed forces GP" means a medical practitioner who is employed on a contract of service by the Ministry of Defence, whether or not as a member of the United Kingdom Armed Forces of Her Majesty; and

"health service body" does not include any person who is to be regarded as a health service body in accordance with regulation 13.

(**a**) Published by the then Scottish Executive as NHS Circular PCA(M)(2001)(17), copies available at http://www.sehd.scot.nhs.uk/pca/pca2001(m)17.htm.

Sub-contracting of clinical matters

62.—(1) Subject to sub-paragraph (2), the contractor may not sub-contract any of its rights or duties under the contract in relation to clinical matters unless—

  (a) in all cases, it has taken reasonable steps to satisfy itself that—

   (i) it is reasonable in all the circumstances; and

   (ii) the proposed sub-contractor person is qualified and competent to provide the service; and

  (b) it has notified the Health Board of its intention to sub-contract as soon as reasonably practicable before the date on which the proposed sub-contract is intended to come into force.

(2) Sub-paragraph (1)(b) does not apply to a contract for services with a health care professional for the provision by that person of clinical services.

(3) The notification referred to in sub-paragraph (1)(b) must include—

  (a) the name and address of the proposed sub-contractor;

  (b) the duration of the proposed sub-contract;

  (c) the services to be covered;

  (d) the address of any premises to be used for the provision of services ; and

  (e) whether the sub-contractor, if that sub-contractor were a contractor, would have sufficient involvement in patient care in terms of section 17L(3) and (4) of the Act(**a**).

(4) Following receipt of a notice in accordance with sub-paragraph (1)(b), the Health Board may request such further information relating to the proposed sub-contract as appears to it to be reasonable and the contractor must supply such information promptly.

(5) The contractor will not proceed with the sub-contract or, if it has already taken effect, must take appropriate steps to terminate it, where, within 28 days of receipt of the notice referred to in sub-paragraph (1)(b), the Health Board has served notice of objection to the sub-contract on the grounds that—

  (a) the sub-contract would—

   (i) put at serious risk the safety of the contractor's patients; or

   (ii) put the Board at risk of material financial loss;

  (b) the sub-contractor would be unable to meet the contractor's obligations under the contract; or

  (c) the sub-contractor would not have sufficient involvement in patient care in terms of section 17L(3) and (4) of the Act, if that sub-contractor were a contractor.

(6) Where the Health Board objects to a proposed sub-contract in accordance with sub-paragraph (5), it must include with the notice of objection a statement in writing of the reasons for its objections.

(7) Sub-paragraphs (1) and (3) to (6) also apply in relation to any renewal or material variation of a sub-contract in relation to clinical matters.

(8) Where a Health Board does not object to a proposed sub-contract under sub-paragraph (5), the parties to the contract will be deemed to have agreed a variation of the contract which has the effect of adding to the list of practice premises any premises whose address was notified to it under sub-paragraph (3)(d) and paragraph 94 (1) does not apply.

(9) A contract with a sub-contractor must prohibit the sub-contractor from sub-contracting the clinical services it has agreed with the contractor to provide.

(**a**) Section 17L was substituted by section 39(1) of the Tobacco and Primary Medical Services (Scotland) Act 2010 (asp 3).

(10) The contractor may not sub contract any of its rights or duties under the contract in relation to the provision of essential services to a company, partnership or limited liability partnership—

(a) owned wholly or partly by the contractor, or by any former or current employee of, or partner or member of the contractor;

(b) formed by or on behalf of the contractor, or from which it derives or may derive a pecuniary benefit; or

(c) formed by or on behalf of a former or current employee of, or partner or partner or member of the contractor, or from which such a person derives or may derive a pecuniary benefit,

where that company, partnership or limited liability partnership is or was formed wholly or partly for the purpose of avoiding the restrictions on the sale of goodwill of a medical practice in section 35 of the Act(**a**) or any regulations made wholly or partly under that section.

PART 5

DATA PROTECTION, RECORDS, INFORMATION, NOTIFICATIONS AND RIGHTS OF ENTRY

Interpretation – general

63.—(1) For the purposes of this Part—

"electronic patient records" means records of the contractor's attendance on its patients created by way of data entries on a computer and electronically held and controlled by the contractor;

"patient records" means records of the contractor's attendance on and treatment of its patients created by way of electronic patient records or on forms supplied by the Health Board to the contractor;

"practice data" means data about a contractor's practice and which may include any information or data about employees, sub-contractors, remuneration, finances, workloads, and contracts other than personal data within patient records.

(2) No provision of this Part is to be construed as creating a duty, obligation or right which is contrary to any duty, obligation or right created by the 1998 Act(**b**) or any directly applicable EU instrument relating to data protection.

Meaning of data controller etc.

64.—(1) The meaning of "data controller", "personal data", "processing" and "supervisory authority" is to be construed in accordance with the 1998 Act.

(2) The meaning of "data controller", "data protection officer", "personal data", "processing" and "supervisory authority" is to be construed in accordance with the GDPR(**c**).

(3) Sub-paragraph (1) ceases to have effect on 25th May 2018.

Roles, responsibilities and obligations – general

65.—(1) The Health Board and the contractor, when processing any data under this Part, must comply with any relevant direction, or guidance issued by the Scottish Ministers.

(**a**) Section 35 was substituted by section 34(2) of the National Health Service (Primary Care) Act 1997 (c.46) and amended by paragraph 1 of schedule 1 of the Primary Medical Services (Scotland) Act 2004 (asp 1).
(**b**) 1998 c.29.
(**c**) OJ L 119, 4.5.2016, p.1-88.

(2) The Health Board and the contractor must include within the contract—
(a) terms which have the effect of the obligations mentioned in paragraphs 65 and 66; and
(b) a term that requires the Health Board and the contractor to act jointly as data controllers in relation to the processing of patient records.

Contractor's obligations – records etc.

66. The contractor must—
(a) take all reasonable steps to ensure the accuracy of patient records;
(b) verify the accuracy of any templates and notices provided to it by the Health Board in accordance with paragraph 67(b), and once verified, use such templates and notices;
(c) comply with the Health Board's current policies concerning data security, personal data or IT security notified by the Health Board to the contractor under paragraph 67(c);
(d) maintain a record of all of the contractor's processing activities carried out in performance of the contract and make the records available to the Health Board on request; and
(e) ensure that any person under its direction who has access to patient records has undergone adequate data protection training.

Health Board Obligations – records etc.

67. The Health Board must—
(a) take all reasonable steps to confirm the accuracy of patient records provided to or accessed by it;
(b) provide to the contractor, guidance, templates, and privacy notices, relating to the contractor's processing of personal data and the contractor's maintenance of a record in accordance with sub-paragraph 66(d);
(c) notify the contractor timeously of its current policies regarding data security, personal data security and IT security processes;
(d) maintain a record of its processing activities carried out in relation to a contractor's patient records;
(e) ensure that any of its employees who have access to the contractor's patient records and practice data has undergone adequate data protection training; and
(f) make available appropriate data protection training to the contractor and its employees.

Records

68.—(1) The contractor must keep adequate patient records of its attendance on and treatment of its patients and must do so—
(a) on forms to be supplied to it for that purpose by the Health Board;
(b) with the written consent of the Health Board, by way of electronic patient records; or
(c) in a combination of those two ways.

(2) The contractor must include in patient records referred to in sub-paragraph (1) clinical reports sent in accordance with paragraph 6 of schedule 6 or from any other health care professional who has provided clinical services to a person on its list of patients.

(3) The consent of the Health Board required by sub-paragraph (1)(b) must not be withheld or withdrawn provided the Health Board is satisfied, and continues to be satisfied, that—
(a) the contractor ensures that the computer system upon which the contractor proposes to keep the electronic patient records is accredited by the Scottish Ministers or another person on their behalf as suitable for that purpose in accordance with a relevant standard issued by the Scottish Ministers;

(b) the security measures, audit and system management functions incorporated into the computer system as accredited in accordance with sub-paragraph (a) have been enabled; and

(c) the contract signed by the contractor contains an obligation requiring the contractor to have regard to any guidelines concerning good practice in the keeping of electronic patient records issued by the Scottish Ministers and notified in writing to the contractor by the Health Board.

(4) Where a patient's records are electronic patient records, the contractor must, as soon as possible following a request from the Health Board, allow the Health Board to access the information recorded on the contractor's computer system by means of the audit function referred to in sub-paragraph (3)(b), to the extent necessary for the Board to confirm that the audit function is enabled and functioning correctly.

(5) The contractor must send the complete patient record relating to a person mentioned in this sub-paragraph to the Health Board—

(a) where a person on its list dies, before the end of a period of 14 days beginning with the date on which it was informed by the Health Board of the death, or (in any other case) before the end of the period of one month beginning with the date on which it learned of the death; or

(b) in any other case where the person is no longer registered with the contractor, as soon as possible, at the request of the Health Board.

(6) To the extent that a patient's records are electronic patient records, the contractor complies with sub-paragraph (5) if it sends to the Health Board a copy of those records—

(a) in written form; or

(b) with the written consent of the Health Board, in any other form.

(7) The consent of the Health Board to the transmission of information other than in written form for the purposes of sub-paragraph (6)(b) shall not be withheld or withdrawn provided the Health Board is satisfied, and continues to be satisfied, with—

(a) the contractor's proposals as to how the record will be transmitted;

(b) the contractor's proposals as to the format of the transmitted record;

(c) how the contractor will ensure that the record received by the Health Board is identical to that transmitted; and

(d) how a written copy of the record can be produced by the Health Board.

(8) A contractor with electronic patient records must not disable, or attempt to disable, either the security measures or the audit and system management functions referred to in sub-paragraph (3)(b).

Processing and access of data

69.—(1) Subject to paragraphs (2) and (4), the contractor must, on the request of the Health Board—

(a) allow the Health Board to access practice data and patient records;

(b) produce or disclose practice data and data within patient records to the Health Board or to any person authorised in writing by the Health Board; and

(c) produce or disclose any other information to the Health Board which is reasonably required in connection with the Health Board's functions.

(2) A request under sub-paragraph (1) must be made—

(a) after consideration of whether the relevant information could be so provided in compliance with the 1998 Act, and any directly applicable EU instrument relating to data protection;

(b) in accordance with directions given to the Health Board by the Scottish Ministers under section 2(5) of the Act that have been consulted upon by a body representative of general medical practitioners providing primary medical services in accordance with a general medical services contract or a section 17C arrangement; and

(c) for a purpose mentioned in sub-paragraph (3).

(3) The purposes mentioned in sub-paragraph (2)(c) are—

(a) medical diagnosis of or provision of healthcare to patients;

(b) the planning, including workforce planning, and management of health and social care services; or

(c) where information is reasonably required in connection with the contract.

(4) The contractor must produce any information relating to a request made in accordance with sub-paragraph (1)(b)—

(a) by such date as has been agreed as reasonable between the contractor and the Health Board; or

(b) in the absence of such agreement, within 28 days of the request being made.

(5) In this paragraph—

(a) "access" includes access by way of any computerised system, integrated information management and technology system or software; and

(b) "disclose" includes the provision of information by electronic means.

Data protection officer

70.—(1) The Health Board must appoint a jointly designated data protection officer where it has agreed to do so with the contractor.

(2) Where a jointly designated data protection officer mentioned in sub-paragraph (1) has not been appointed, the contractor must nominate a person with responsibility for working together with the Health Board's data protection officer in matters relating to the protection of personal data and the implementation of the Health Board's guidance, templates and policies on such matters set out under paragraph 67(b).

GP IT Services

71.—(1) The Health Board will provide, maintain and where necessary, upgrade any integrated information management and technology systems used by the contractor for provision of services under the contract and any telecommunication links between these systems and the systems used by the Health Board, a Special Health Board, the Agency, or Healthcare Improvement Scotland, in accordance with any relevant guidance (including standards) issued from time to time by the Scottish Ministers.

(2) The Health Board and contractor must take into account any relevant guidance issued by the Scottish Ministers for the purposes of this paragraph and this Part.

(3) On the expiry or termination of the contract, the contractor must immediately return to the Health Board any integrated information management and technology systems and telecommunication links purchased or provided by the Health Board for the purposes of this paragraph in its possession unless otherwise agreed between the Health Board and contractor.

Patient online appointment services

72.—(1) A contractor must provide its registered patients with—

(a) an optional online appointment service;

(b) an optional online repeat prescription service; and

(c) an optional online repeat prescription information service,

in a manner which is capable of being electronically integrated with the computer systems of the contractor's practice and using appropriate systems authorised by the Health Board.

(2) The requirements in sub-paragraph (1) do not apply where the contractor does not have access to computer systems and software which would enable it to provide the services listed in that sub-paragraph.

(3) If the contractor provides an optional online appointment service, the contractor must regularly consider whether it is desirable, in order to meet the reasonable needs of its registered patients, to increase the proportion of appointments which are made available to registered patients through that service and if it is so desirable, to increase the proportion of appointments accordingly.

(4) If a contractor provides any of the services referred to in sub-paragraph (1), the contractor must promote that service to its registered patients—

(a) in practice leaflets in accordance with paragraph 11 of schedule 8; and

(b) if the contactor has a website, on that website.

(5) In this paragraph—

(a) "online appointment service" means a facility which allows patients to book view, amend and cancel appointments online;

(b) "repeat prescription service" means a facility which allows patients to order repeat prescriptions for drugs, medicines or appliances online; and

(c) "online repeat prescription information service" means a facility which allows patients to view online, and print, a list of any drugs, medicines or appliances in respect of which the patient has a repeat prescription.

Confidentiality of personal data

73. The contractor must nominate a person with responsibility for practices and procedures relating to the confidentiality of personal data held by it and also data protection generally.

Practice leaflet

74. The contractor must—

(a) compile a document (in this paragraph called a practice leaflet) which includes the information specified in schedule 8;

(b) review its practice leaflet at least once in every period of twelve months and make any amendments necessary to maintain its accuracy; and

(c) make available a copy of the leaflet, and any subsequent updates, to its patients and prospective patients.

Inquiries about prescriptions and referrals

75.—(1) The contractor must, subject to sub-paragraphs (2) and (3), sufficiently answer any inquires whether oral or in writing from the Health Board concerning—

(a) any prescription form issued by a prescriber;

(b) the considerations by reference to which prescribers issue such forms;

(c) the referral by or on behalf of the contractor of any patient to any other services provided under the Act; or

(d) the considerations by which the contractor makes such referrals or provides for them to be made on its behalf.

(2) An inquiry referred to in sub-paragraph (1) may only be made for the purpose either of obtaining information to assist the Health Board to discharge its functions or of assisting the contractor in the discharge of its obligations under the contract.

(3) The contractor is not obliged to answer any inquiry referred to in sub-paragraph (1) unless it is made—

(a) in the case of sub-paragraph (1)(a) or (b), by an appropriately qualified health care professional;

(b) in the case of sub-paragraph (1)(c) or (d), by an appropriately qualified medical practitioner,

appointed in either case by the Health Board to assist the Board in the exercise of its functions under this paragraph and that person produces, on request, written evidence that the person is authorised by the Health Board to make such an inquiry on its behalf.

Provision of information to a medical officer etc

76.—(1) The contractor is to, if it is satisfied that the patient has given explicit consent—

(a) supply in writing to any person specified in sub-paragraph (3), within such reasonable period as that person may specify, such clinical information as any of the persons mentioned in sub-paragraph (3)(a) to (d) considers relevant about a patient to whom the contractor or a person acting on behalf of the contractor has issued or has refused to issue a medical certificate; and

(b) answer any inquiries by any person mentioned in sub-paragraph (3) about—

(i) a prescription form or medical certificate issued or created by, or on behalf of, the contractor; or

(ii) any statement which the contractor or a person acting on behalf of that contractor has made in a report.

(2) For the purposes of being satisfied that a patient has given explicit consent, a contractor may rely on an assurance in writing from any person mentioned to sub-paragraph (3) that the explicit consent of the patient has been obtained, unless the contractor has reason to believe that the patient does not consent.

(3) For the purposes of sub-paragraphs (1) and (2), the persons are—

(a) a medical officer;

(b) a nursing officer;

(c) an occupational therapist;

(d) a physiotherapist; or

(e) an officer of the Department for Work and Pensions who is acting on behalf of, and at the direction of, any person specified in paragraphs (a) to (d).

(4) In this paragraph—

(a) "medical officer" means a medical practitioner who is—

(i) employed or engaged by the Department for Work and Pensions; or

(ii) provided by an organisation under a contract entered into with the Secretary of State for Work and Pensions;

(b) "nursing officer" means a health care professional who is registered on the Nursing and Midwifery Register and—

(i) employed or engaged by the Department for Work and Pensions; or

(ii) provided by an organisation under a contract entered into with the Secretary of State for Work and Pensions;

(c) "occupational therapist" means a health care professional who is registered in the part of the register maintained by the Health Professions Council under article 5 of the Health and Social Work Professions Order 2001(**a**) relating to occupational therapists and—

    (i) employed or engaged by the Department for Work and Pensions; or

    (ii) provided by an organisation under a contract entered into with the Secretary of State for Work and Pensions; and

(d) "physiotherapist" means a health care professional who is registered in the part of the register maintained by the Health Professions Council under article 5 of the Health and Social Work Professions Order 2001 relating to physiotherapists and—

    (i) employed or engaged by the Department for Work and Pensions; or

    (ii) provided by an organisation under a contract entered into with the Secretary of State for Work and Pensions.

Annual return and review

77.—(1) The contractor must submit an annual return relating to the contract to the Health Board which requires the same categories of information from all persons who hold contracts with that Board.

(2) One such return may be requested by the Health Board at any time during each financial year in relation to such period (not including any period covered by a previous annual return) as may be specified in the request.

(3) The contractor must submit the completed return to the Health Board—

(a) by such date as has been agreed as reasonable between the contractor and the Health Board; or

(b) in the absence of such agreement, within 28 days of the request being made.

(4) Without prejudice to the generality of sub-paragraph (1), the contractor must include in the annual return a statement confirming—

(a) that the contractor satisfies the requirements of regulations 10 and 11;

(b) that neither the contractor nor any member or shareholder of the contractor falls within sub-paragraph 103(2);

(c) the details specified in sub-paragraph (5);

(d) that any sub-contractor satisfies the requirements of paragraph 62(3)(e); and,

(e) any further details as the Health Board considers appropriate.

(5) The contractor must provide details of each partner, member, shareholder, or medical practitioner (if the contractor is that medical practitioner), who falls within regulation 11(2)(a) or (b) ("a relevant individual") confirming for each relevant individual whether—

(a) they satisfy—

    (i) the requirement to have sufficient involvement in patient care under regulation 11(1), and if so whether they fall within regulation 11(2)(a), (3) or (4); or

    (ii) the requirements in regulation 11(8);

(b) they comply with regulation 10;

(c) they fall within paragraph 103(2); and

(d) they are a medical practitioner.

(6) Following receipt of the return referred to in sub-paragraph (1), the Health Board must arrange with the contractor an annual review of its performance in relation to the contract.

(**a**) S.I. 2002/254, as retitled by section 213(6) of the Health and Social Care Act 2012 (c.7). Article 5 was amended by S.I. 2009/1182. The title of this Order is the Health and Social Work Profession Order 2002 but it is cited as the Health and Social Work Profession Order 2001 in accordance with section 213(4) of the Health and Social care Act 2012 c.7.

(7) Either the contractor or the Health Board may, if it wishes to do so, invite the area medical committee for the area of the Health Board to participate in the annual review.

(8) The Health Board must prepare a draft record of the review referred to in sub-paragraph (2) for comment by the contractor and, having regard to such comments, must produce a final written record of the review.

(9) A copy of the final record referred to in sub-paragraph (8) must be sent to the contractor.

(10) In this paragraph, "financial year" means the twelve months ending with 31st March.

Notifications to the Health Board

78. In addition to any requirements of notification elsewhere in the Regulations, the contractor must notify the Health Board in writing as soon as reasonably practicable, of—
- (a) any serious incident that, in the reasonable opinion of the contractor, affects or is likely to affect the contractor's performance of its obligations under the contract;
- (b) any circumstances which give rise to the Health Board's right to terminate the contract under paragraph 101,102 or 103(1);
- (c) any appointments system which it proposes to operate and the proposed discontinuance of any such system;
- (d) any change of which it is aware in the address of a registered patient; and
- (e) the death of any patient of which it is aware.

Notifications to the Health Board

79. The contractor must, unless it is impracticable for it to do so, notify the Health Board in writing within 28 days of any occurrence requiring a change in the information about it published by the Health Board in accordance with regulations made under section 2C(3) of the Act (Function of Health Boards: primary medical services)(**a**).

Notifications to the Health Board

80. The contractor must notify the Health Board in writing of any person other than a registered patient or a person whom it has accepted as a temporary resident to whom it has provided the essential services described in regulation 18(6) or (8) within the period of 28 days beginning on the day that the services were provided.

Notice provisions specific to a contract with a company

81.—(1) A contractor which is a company must give notice in writing to the Health Board without delay when—
- (a) any share in the contractor is transmitted or transferred (including legally or beneficially) to another person on a date after the contract has come into force, if the contractor's contract was entered into prior to 22nd December 2010;
- (b) a member of the company ceases to be a member of the company or informs the other members of the company that that person intends to cease to be a member of the company, (and the notice must state the date upon which they ceased, or will cease, to be a member, of the company), if the contractor's contract was entered into on or after 22nd December 2010;
- (c) a person becomes a member of the company, if the contractor's contract was entered into on or after 22nd December 2010;

(**a**) Section 2C was inserted into the Act by section 1(2) of the Primary Medical Services (Scotland) Act 2004 (asp 1).

(d) a, director or secretary of the company ceases to be a director or secretary of the company or informs the company that that person intends to cease to be a director or secretary of the company, and the notice must state the date upon which they ceased, or will cease, to be a director or secretary of the company;

(e) a new director or secretary becomes a director or secretary of the company;

(f) the company passes a resolution or a court of competent jurisdiction makes an order that the contractor be wound up;

(g) circumstances arise which might entitle a creditor or a court to appoint a receiver, administrator or administrative receiver for the contractor;

(h) circumstances arise which would enable the court to make a winding up order in respect of the contractor; or

(i) the contractor is unable to pay its debts within the meaning of section 123 of the Insolvency Act 1986(**a**).

(2) A notice under sub-paragraph (1)(a) or (c) must—

(a) confirm that the new member, shareholder, or, as the case may be, the personal representative of a deceased shareholder—

(i) satisfies the conditions specified in regulation 11(1) or (9);

(ii) meets the further conditions in regulation 10; and

(iii) does not fall within paragraph 103(2); and

(b) state the date the new member or shareholder became a member or shareholder of the company.

(3) A notice under sub-paragraph (1)(e) must—

(a) state the date the new director or secretary became a director or secretary of the company; and

(b) confirm that the new director or, as the case may be, secretary does not fall within paragraph 103(2).

Notice provisions specific to a contract with persons practising in partnership

82.—(1) A contractor which is a partnership must give notice in writing to the Health Board without delay when—

(a) a partner leaves or informs the other members of the partnership that the partner intends to leave the partnership; or

(b) a new partner joins the partnership.

(2) A notice under sub-paragraph (1)(a) must state the date upon which the partner left or will leave the partnership.

(3) A notice under sub-paragraph (1)(b) must—

(a) state the date that the new partner joined the partnership;

(b) confirm that the new partner satisfies the conditions specified in regulations 10 and 11(1) or (8) and does not fall within paragraph 103(2); and

(c) state whether the new partner is a general or a limited partner.

(**a**) 1986 c.45.

Notice provisions specific to a contract with persons practising in a limited liability partnership

83.—(1) A contractor which is a limited liability partnership must give notice in writing to the Health Board without delay when—

(a) a member ceases to be a member, or informs the other members of the partnership that the member intends to cease to be a member of the partnership; or

(b) a new member joins the partnership.

(2) A notice under sub-paragraph (1)(a) must state the date upon which the member ceased, or will cease, to be a member of the partnership.

(3) A notice under sub-paragraph (1)(b) must—

(a) state the date that the new member joined the limited liability partnership; and

(b) confirm that the new member satisfies the conditions specified in regulations 10 and 11(1) or (8) and does not fall within paragraph 103(2).

Notification of deaths

84.—(1) The contractor must report, in writing, to the Health Board, the death on its practice premises of any patient no later than the end of the first working day after the date on which the death occurred.

(2) The report must include—

(a) the patient's full name;

(b) the patient's National Health Service number where known;

(c) the date and place of death;

(d) a brief description of the circumstances, as known, surrounding the death;

(e) the name of any medical practitioner or other person treating the patient whilst on the practice premises; and

(f) the name, where known, of any other person who was present at the time of the death.

(3) The contractor must send a copy of the report referred to in sub-paragraph (1) to any other Health Board in whose area the deceased was resident at the time of the patient's death.

Notifications to patients following variation of the contract

85. Where the contract is varied in accordance with Part 8 of this schedule and, as a result of that variation—

(a) there is to be a change in the range of services provided to the contractor's registered patients; or

(b) patients who are on the contractor's list of patients are to be removed from that list,

the Health Board must notify those patients in writing of the variation and its effect and inform them of the steps they can take to obtain elsewhere the services in question or, as the case may be, register elsewhere for the provision of essential services (or their equivalent).

Entry and inspection by the Health Board

86.—(1) Subject to the conditions in sub-paragraph (2), the contractor must allow persons authorised in writing by the Health Board to enter and inspect the practice premises at any reasonable time.

(2) The conditions referred to in sub-paragraph (1) are that—

(a) reasonable notice of the intended entry has been given;

(b) written evidence of the authority of the person seeking entry is produced to the contractor on request; and

(c) entry is not made to any premises or part of the premises used as residential accommodation without the consent of the resident.

(3) Either the contractor or the Health Board may, if it wishes to do so, invite the area medical committee for the area of the Board to be present at an inspection of the practice premises which takes place under this paragraph.

PART 6

COMPLAINTS

Complaints procedure

87. The contractor must have arrangements in place which operate in accordance with section 15 of the Patient Rights (Scotland) Act 2011(**a**), and any regulations or directions made under that Act.

Co-operation with investigations

88.—(1) The contractor must co-operate with—

(a) any investigation of a complaint in relation to any matter reasonably connected with the provision of services under the contract undertaken by—

   (i) the Health Board; or

   (ii) the Scottish Public Services Ombudsman;

(b) any investigation of a complaint by a NHS body or local authority which relates to a patient or former patient of the contractor.

(2) In sub-paragraph (1)—

"NHS body" means, in Scotland, any Health Board or Special Health Board or the Agency, in England and Wales, the National Health Service Commissioning Board(**b**) or a Local Health Board, and, in Northern Ireland a Health and Social Care trust or Regional Health and Social Care Board;

"local authority" means—

(a) a council constituted under section 2 of the Local Government etc. (Scotland) Act 1994 (constitution of councils)(**c**);

(b) any of the bodies listed in section 1 of the Local Authority Social Services Act 1970 (local authorities)(**d**);

(c) the Council of the Isles of Scilly; or

(d) a council of a county or county borough in Wales.

(3) The co-operation required by sub-paragraph (1) includes—

(a) answering questions reasonably put to the contractor by the NHS body, local authority or Scottish Public Services Ombudsman;

(b) providing any information relating to the complaint reasonably required by the NHS body, local authority or Scottish Public Services Ombudsman; and

---

(**a**) 2011 asp 5.
(**b**) Established under section 1H of the National Health Service Act 2006 (c.41). Section 1H was inserted by section 9(1) of the Health and Social Care Act 2012 (c.7)- and was amended by S.I. 2012/1831.
(**c**) 1994 c.39. Section 2 was amended by paragraph 232(1) of the Environment Act 1995 (c.25).
(**d**) 1970 c.42. Section 1 was amended by S.I. 2016/413.

(c) attending any meeting to consider the complaint (if held at a reasonably accessible place and at a reasonable hour, and due notice has been given) if the contractor's presence at the meeting is reasonably required by the NHS body, local authority or Scottish Public Services Ombudsman.

PART 7

DISPUTE RESOLUTION

Local resolution of contract disputes: local dispute resolution process

89.—(1) For the purposes of this paragraph —

"local medical committee" means a local representative committee which represents the interests of general medical practitioners providing primary medical services in its locality and which is identified and recognised by the British Medical Association as a local medical committee on the British Medical Association's website(a) as updated or replaced from time to time;

"local resolution approved mediator" means a mediator who is on the list of trained mediators kept in accordance with sub-paragraph (2) by a Health Board ("the first Health Board") (other than the Health Board who is a party to the relevant contract ("the Second Health Board")) which is requested by the Second Health Board to appoint a local resolution panel and which mediator is chosen by the local resolution panel in accordance with sub-paragraph (6);

"local resolution approved mediator functions" means the functions of—

(a) facilitating, co-ordinating and mediating communication between the parties to a dispute arising out of or in connection with a contract with a view to helping the parties to reach a voluntary resolution to their dispute;

(b) assisting the parties to explore options for negotiating a resolution to the dispute; and

(c) providing recommendations to facilitate resolution of the contractual dispute and reporting to the area medical committee, the local resolution panel and the parties to the dispute in accordance with sub-paragraph (9).

"local resolution panel" means a committee or a subcommittee of the first Health Board appointed by the first Health Board at the request of the second Health Board which must consist of—

(a) a person representative of patients in the area of the second Health Board;

(b) a person representative of the local medical committee, in the area of the second Health Board;

(c) a person who is an employee of the first Health Board. and

"local resolution report" means the written report provided by a local resolution approved mediator in accordance with sub-paragraph (9);

(2) Every Health Board will keep a list of trained mediators who are also employees of the Health Board or available to be engaged by the Health Board and who the Health Board is satisfied are capable of performing the local resolution approved mediator functions.

(3) In the case of any dispute arising out of or in connection with the contract—

(a) the contractor and the first Health Board must make every reasonable effort to communicate and co-operate with each other with a view to resolving the dispute in accordance with the local dispute resolution process, before referring the dispute for determination in accordance with the NHS dispute resolution procedure (or, where applicable, before commencing court proceedings); and

---

(a) https://www.bma.org.uk/about-us/how-we-work/local-representation/local-medical-committees.

(b) neither the contractor nor the first Health Board may refer the dispute for determination in accordance with the NHS dispute resolution procedure (or, where applicable, before commencing court proceedings) until the local dispute resolution process has been completed.

(4) Either party to the contract may commence the local dispute resolution process by serving written notice on—

(a) the other party to the contract; and

(b) the area medical committee for the second Health Board's area.

(5) The written notice referred to in sub-paragraph (4) must set out—

(a) the issue in dispute which must arise out of or be in connection with the contract;

(b) contact details for the parties to the contract; and

(c) any background information which may be reasonably required by a local resolution approved mediator to perform their functions.

(6) Upon receipt of the notice referred to in sub-paragraph (4)—

(a) the Second Health Board must request that the First Health Board convene a local resolution panel; and

(b) that local resolution panel must choose, from the list of local resolution approved mediators, a local resolution approved mediator whom the panel considers capable of performing the local resolution approved mediator functions in relation to the dispute.

(7) The parties must provide the local resolution approved mediator and each other with any information which may reasonably be required to facilitate the resolution of the dispute and to enable the local resolution approved mediator to perform their local resolution approved mediator functions.

(8) The local resolution approved mediator must complete their local resolution approved mediator functions within three months from service of the notice referred to in sub-paragraph (4).

(9) Within the period specified in sub-paragraph (8), the local resolution approved mediator must provide a written report to the parties, the area medical committee and the local resolution panel referred to in sub-paragraph (4) which sets out the following—

(a) any agreement reached between the parties;

(b) the local resolution approved mediator's recommendation on how to resolve any issues still in dispute; and

(c) confirmation that the local dispute resolution process has been completed.

(10) The local resolution report may be considered by the Scottish Ministers in the event that either party wishes to refer the dispute to the Scottish Ministers for determination in accordance with paragraphs 90 or 91.

Dispute resolution: non-NHS contracts

90.—(1) In the case of a contract which is not an NHS contract, any dispute arising out of or in connection with the contract, except matters dealt with under the complaints procedure pursuant to Part 6 of this schedule, may be referred for consideration and determination to the Scottish Ministers, if—

(a) the Health Board so wishes and the contractor has agreed in writing; or

(b) the contractor so wishes (even if the Health Board does not agree).

(2) In the case of a dispute referred to the Scottish Ministers under sub-paragraph (1)—

(a) the procedure to be followed is the NHS dispute resolution procedure; and

(b) the parties agree to be bound by any determination made by the adjudicator.

NHS dispute resolution procedure

91.—(1) Subject to sub-paragraph (2), the procedure specified in the following sub-paragraphs and paragraph 92 applies in the case of any dispute arising out of, or in connection with, the contract which is referred to the Scottish Ministers—

(a) in accordance with section 17A(4) of the Act(**a**) (where the contract is a NHS contract); or

(b) in accordance with paragraph 90(1) (where the contract is not a NHS contract).

(2) In the case where—

(a) a dispute is referred to the Scottish Ministers in accordance with regulation 12(1) (pre-contract disputes); or

(b) a contractor (or contractors) refers a matter for determination in accordance with paragraph 33(1) or (2),

the procedure specified in the following sub-paragraphs and paragraph 92 is modified as mentioned in regulation 12 or, as the case may be, paragraph 33.

(3) Any party wishing to refer a dispute as mentioned in sub-paragraph (1) must send to the Scottish Ministers a written request for dispute resolution which includes or is accompanied by—

(a) the names and addresses of the parties to the dispute;

(b) a copy of the contract; and

(c) a brief statement describing the nature and circumstances of the dispute.

(4) Any party wishing to refer a dispute as mentioned in sub-paragraph (1) must send the request under sub-paragraph (3) within a period of 3 years beginning with the date on which the matter giving rise to the dispute happened or should reasonably have come to the attention of the party wishing to refer the dispute.

(5) The Scottish Ministers may determine the dispute themselves or, if they consider it appropriate, appoint a panel consisting of three persons (referred to as "the panel") to consider and determine the dispute.

(6) Before reaching a decision as to who should determine the dispute under sub-paragraph (5), the Scottish Ministers must, within a period of 7 days beginning with the date on which the dispute was referred to them, send a written request to the parties to make in writing, within a specified period, any representations which they may wish to make about the matter under dispute.

(7) The Scottish Ministers must send, with the notice given under sub-paragraph (6), to the party other than the one which referred the matter to dispute resolution, a copy of any document by which the matter was referred to dispute resolution.

(8) The Scottish Ministers must give a copy of any representations received from a party to the other party and must in each case request (in writing) a party to whom a copy of the representations is given to make within a specified period any written observations which it wishes to make on those representations.

(9) Following receipt of any representations from the parties or, if earlier, at the end of the period for making such representations specified in the request sent under sub-paragraph (6) or (8), the Scottish Ministers must, if they decide to appoint a panel to hear the dispute—

(a) inform the parties in writing of the names of the persons whom they have appointed on the panel; and

(b) pass to the panel any documents received from the parties under or pursuant to paragraph (3), (6) or (8).

(**a**) Section 17A was inserted by section 30 of the National Health Service and Community Care Act 1990 (c.19). Section 17A was moved under a new heading entitled "NHS Contracts" by section 31 of the National Health Service (Primary Care) Act 1997 (c.46).

(10) For the purpose of assisting it in its consideration of the matter, the adjudicator may—

    (a) invite representatives of the parties to appear before the adjudicator to make oral representations either together or, with the agreement of the parties, separately, and may in advance provide the parties with a list of matters or questions to which it wishes them to give special consideration; or

    (b) consult other persons whose expertise the adjudicator considers will assist the adjudicator in the adjudicator's consideration of the matter.

(11) Where the adjudicator consults another person under sub-paragraph (10)(b), the adjudicator must notify the parties accordingly in writing and, where the adjudicator considers that the interests of any party might be substantially affected by the result of the consultation, the adjudicator must give to the parties such opportunity as it considers reasonable in the circumstances to make observations on those results.

(12) In considering the matter, the adjudicator must consider—

    (a) any written representations made in response to a request under sub-paragraph (6) but only if they are made within the specified period;

    (b) any written observations made in response to a request under sub-paragraph (8), but only if they are made within the specified period;

    (c) any oral representations made in response to an invitation under sub-paragraph (10)(a);

    (d) the results of any consultation under sub-paragraph (10)(b); and

    (e) any observations made in accordance with an opportunity given under sub-paragraph (11).

(13) In this paragraph, "specified period" means such period as the Scottish Ministers specify in the request sent under sub-paragraph (6) or (8), being not less than 2, nor more than 4 weeks beginning with the date on which the request is sent, but the adjudicator may, if the adjudicator considers that there is good reason for doing so, extend any such period (even after it has expired) and where it does so, a reference in this paragraph to the specified period is to the period as so extended.

(14) Subject to the other provisions of this paragraph and paragraph 92 and to any agreement by the parties, the adjudicator is to have wide discretion in determining the procedure of the dispute resolution to ensure the just, expeditious, economical and final determination of the dispute.

(15) Where the adjudicator is a panel, any decision or determination by the panel for the purposes of this paragraph and paragraph 92 may be by a majority.

Determination of dispute

92.—(1) The adjudicator must record its determination, and the reasons for it, in writing and must give notice of the determination (including the record of the reasons) to the parties and, in the case where the adjudicator is a panel, to the Scottish Ministers.

(2) Subsections (8) and (9) of section 17A of the Act (NHS contracts), as modified by regulation 13(7)(d) apply in the case of a determination of a reference under paragraph 90(1) as they apply in the case of a determination under subsection (4) of that section.

Interpretation of Part 7

93.—(1) In this Part, "any dispute arising out of or in connection with the contract" includes any dispute arising out of or in connection with the termination of the contract.

(2) Any term of the contract that makes provision in respect of the requirements in this Part will survive even where the contract has terminated.

PART 8

VARIATION AND TERMINATION OF CONTRACTS

Variation of a contract: general

94.—(1) Subject to regulation 31, schedule 2 and paragraphs 62(8) and 108 of this schedule and sub-paragraph (2), no amendment or variation has effect unless it is in writing and signed by or on behalf of the Health Board and the contractor.

(2) In addition to the specific provision made in paragraph 108 the Health Board may vary the contract without the contractor's consent where it—

  (a) is reasonably satisfied that it is necessary to vary the contract so as to comply with relevant legislation; and

  (b) notifies the contractor in writing of the wording of the proposed variation and the date upon which that variation is to take effect.

(3) Where it is reasonably practicable to do so, the date that the proposed variation is to take effect is to be not less than 14 days after the date on which the notice under sub-paragraph (2)(b) is served on the contractor.

(4) In this paragraph "relevant legislation" means—

  (a) the Act;

  (b) the 1998 Act(**a**) or any directly applicable EU instrument relating to data protection;

  (c) the Patient Rights (Scotland) Act 2016(**b**);

  (d) Part 2 of the Health (Tobacco, Nicotine etc. and Care) (Scotland) Act 2016(**c**); and

  (e) any regulations or any direction given by the Scottish Ministers made pursuant to the Acts mentioned in sub-paragraphs (a), (c) and (d).

Variation of a contract: execution

95.—(1) If the contract or any amendment or variation to the contract under paragraph 94(1) is executed in counterpart, each counterpart when executed and delivered is to constitute an original of the contract or amendment or variation to the contract; but both of the counterparts will together constitute the same agreed contract, amendment or variation and no counterpart will be effective until each party has executed and delivered an executed counterpart to the other party.

(2) A counterpart of a contract or an amendment or variation to a contract may be delivered by a party ("the executing party") to the other party by either—

  (a) the executing party printing out and signing the signature pages of the contract or amendment or variation (both the signature page following the last clause and the signature page following any schedule); and

  (b) the executing party scanning those signed signature pages to an electronic file; or

  (c) the executing party (or its legal representative) emailing the files of the scanned signature pages together with a copy of the contract, amendment or variation to the other party.

Termination by agreement

96. The Health Board and the contractor may agree in writing to terminate the contract, and if the parties so agree, they must agree the date upon which that termination should take effect and any further terms upon which the contract should be terminated.

(**a**) 1998 c.29.
(**b**) 2016 asp 14.
(**c**) 2016 asp 14.

Termination on the death of an individual medical practitioner

97.—(1) Where the contract is with an individual medical practitioner and that practitioner dies, the contract will terminate at the end of a period of seven days after the date of the practitioner's death unless, before the end of that period—

(a) the Health Board has agreed in writing with the contractor's personal representative that the contract should continue for a further period, not exceeding 28 days after the end of the period of seven days; and

(b) the contractor's personal representative has consented in writing to the Health Board employing or supplying one or more general medical practitioners to assist in the provision of clinical services under the contract throughout the period for which it continues.

(2) In sub-paragraph (1), "general medical practitioner" has the same meaning as in regulation 5(1).

(3) Sub-paragraph (1) does not affect any other rights to terminate the contract which the Health Board may have under paragraphs 102 to 106.

Termination by the contractor

98.—(1) A contractor may terminate the contract by serving notice in writing on the Health Board at any time.

(2) Where the contractor serves notice pursuant to sub-paragraph (1), the contract will, subject to sub-paragraph (3), terminate six months after the date on which the notice is served ("the termination date"), save that if the termination date is not the last calendar day of a month, the contract will instead terminate on the last calendar day of the month in which the termination date falls.

(3) Where the contractor is an individual medical practitioner, sub-paragraph (2) applies to the contractor, save that the reference to "six months" is instead to be to "three months".

(4) This paragraph and paragraph 99 are without prejudice to any other rights to terminate the contract that the contractor may have.

Late payment notices

99.—(1) The contractor may give notice in writing (a "late payment notice") to the Health Board if the Board has failed to make any payments due to the contractor in accordance with a term of the contract that has the effect specified in regulation 26 and the contractor must specify in the late payment notice the payments that the Board has failed to make in accordance with that regulation.

(2) Subject to sub-paragraph (3), the contractor may, at least 28 days after having served a late payment notice, terminate the contract by a further written notice if the Health Board has still failed to make the payments due to the contractor, and that were specified in the late payment notice served on the Health Board pursuant to sub-paragraph (1).

(3) If, following receipt of a late payment notice, the Health Board refers the matter to the NHS dispute resolution procedure within 28 days of the date upon which it is served with the late payment notice, and it notifies the contractor in writing that it has done so within that period of time, the contractor may not terminate the contract pursuant to sub-paragraph (2) until—

(a) there has been a determination of the dispute pursuant to paragraph 92 and that determination permits the contractor to terminate the contract; or

(b) the Health Board ceases to pursue the NHS dispute resolution procedure,

whichever is the sooner.

Termination by the Health Board: general

100. The Health Board may only terminate the contract in accordance with the provision in this Part.

Termination by the Health Board for breach of conditions in regulation 10

101.—(1) The Health Board must serve notice in writing on the contractor terminating the contract with immediate effect where the contractor is an individual medical practitioner but is no longer a general medical practitioner.

(2) Sub-paragraph (3) applies when any of the conditions in regulation 10(1)(b) to (f) are no longer satisfied.

(3) Where this sub-paragraph applies, the Health Board must—

(a) serve notice in writing on the contractor terminating the contract with immediate effect; or

(b) serve notice in writing on the contractor confirming that the Health Board will allow the contract to continue, for a period specified by the Health Board of up to six months ("the interim period").

(4) Before deciding which of the options in sub-paragraph (3) to pursue, the Health Board must consult the area medical committee for its area where it is reasonably practicable to do so.

(5) During the interim period under sub-paragraph (3)(b) the Health Board must, with the consent of the contractor, employ or supply to the contractor one or more general medical practitioners to assist in the provision of clinical services under the contract.

(6) If the contractor—

(a) does not consent to the Health Board employing or supplying a general medical practitioner during the interim period; or

(b) still falls within sub-paragraph (2) at the end of the interim period,

the Health Board must serve notice in writing on the contractor terminating the contract with immediate effect.

Termination by the Health Board for breach of conditions in relation to provision of information about compliance with regulations 5, 6, 7, 10 and 11

102. The Health Board may serve notice in writing on the contractor terminating the contract with immediate effect or from such date as may be specified in the notice if—

(a) in the case of a contract entered into prior to 22nd December 2010, after the contract has been entered into, it comes to the attention of the Health Board that written information provided to the Health Board by the contractor—

(i) before the contract was entered into; or

(ii) pursuant to paragraphs 81(2) or (3) or 82(2),

in relation to the conditions set out in regulations 4 and 5 of the 2004 Regulations as in force at 21st December 2010 (in relation to a compliance with those conditions) and regulations 10 and 11 and confirmation that a person did not fall within paragraph 103(2) was, when given, untrue or inaccurate in a material respect; or

(b) in the case of a contract entered into on or after 22nd December 2010, after the contract has been entered into, it comes to the attention of the Health Board that written information provided to the Health Board by the contractor—

(i) before the contract was entered into; or

(ii) pursuant to paragraphs 81(2) or (3) or 82(2),

in relation to the conditions set out in regulations 4 and 5 of the 2004 Regulations or regulations 5, 6 and 7 of these Regulations (and in relation to compliance with those conditions) and regulations 10 and 11 and confirmation that a person did not fall within paragraph 103(2) was, when given, untrue or inaccurate in a material respect.

Other grounds for termination by the Health Board

103.—(1) The Health Board may serve notice in writing on the contractor terminating the contract with immediate effect, or from such date as may be specified in the notice if the contractor is in breach of regulation 11 or if—

(a) in the case of a contract entered into on or after 22nd December 2010—

    (i) with a medical practitioner, that medical practitioner;

    (ii) with a partnership, any partner or the partnership;

    (iii) with a limited liability partnership, any member or the limited liability partnership; and

    (iv) with a company—

        (aa) the company;

        (bb) any member of the company; or

        (cc) any director or secretary of the company;

or,

(b) in the case of a contract entered into prior to 22nd December 2010—

    (i) with a medical practitioner, that medical practitioner;

    (ii) with a partnership, any partner or the partnership;

    (iii) with a company limited by shares—

        (aa) the company;

        (bb) any person legally and beneficially owning a share of the company; or

        (cc) any director or secretary of the company,

falls within sub-paragraph (2) during the existence of the contract.

(2) A person falls within this sub-paragraph if—

(a) the person has been disqualified;

(b) subject to sub-paragraph (3), the person is disqualified or suspended from practising by any licensing body anywhere in the world other than by—

    (i) a direction under section 32A(2) (applications for interim suspension) or 32B(1) (suspension pending appeal) of the Act(**a**);

    (ii) a Health Board in terms of Regulation 8A of the National Health Service (Primary Medical Services Performers Lists) (Scotland) Regulations 2004(**b**); or

    (iii) any provision in force in England, Wales or Northern Ireland corresponding to the provisions referred to in sub-heads (i) and (ii);

(c) subject to sub-paragraph (4), the person has been dismissed (otherwise than by reason of redundancy) from any employment by a health service body unless before the Health Board has served a notice terminating the contract pursuant to this paragraph, the person is employed by the health service body that dismissed the person or by another health service body;

(d) the person is disqualified from a list unless the person's name has subsequently been included in such a list;

(e) the person has been convicted in the United Kingdom of murder;

(f) the person has been convicted in the United Kingdom of a criminal offence, other than of murder, and has been sentenced to a term of imprisonment of over six months;

(**a**) Sections 32A(2) and 32B(1) were inserted by section 8 of the National Health Service (Amendment) Act 1995 (c.31). Section 32A(2) was amended by paragraph 51 of schedule 4 of the Health Act 1999 (c.8) ("the 1999 Act") and section 26(7) of the Smoking, Health and Social Care (Scotland) Act 2005 (asp 13) ("the 2005 Act"). Section 32B(1) was amended by paragraph 52 of schedule 4 of the 1999 Act, and paragraph 1 of schedule 3 of the 2005 Act.

(**b**) S.S.I. 2004/114. Regulation 8A was inserted by S.S.I. 2011/392.

(g) subject to sub-paragraph (5), the person has been convicted elsewhere of an offence—

    (i) which would, if committed in Scotland, constitute murder; or

    (ii) constitute a criminal offence other than murder, and been sentenced to a term of imprisonment of over six months;

(h) the person has been convicted of an offence referred to in schedule 1 of the Criminal Procedure (Scotland) Act 1995(**a**)or schedule 1 of the Children and Young Persons Act 1933(**b**);

(i) the person has—

    (i) had sequestration of the person's estate awarded or been adjudged bankrupt unless (in either case) the person has been discharged or the bankruptcy order has been annulled;

    (ii) been made the subject of a bankruptcy restrictions order or an interim bankruptcy restrictions order under schedule 4A of the Insolvency Act 1986(**c**) or sections 56A to 56K of the Bankruptcy (Scotland) Act 1985(**d**), or sections 155 to 160 of the Bankruptcy (Scotland) Act 2016(**e**) unless that order has ceased to have effect or has been annulled;

    (iii) made a composition or arrangement with, or granted a trust deed for, the person's creditors unless the person has been discharged in respect of it; or

    (iv) been wound up under Part IV of the Insolvency Act 1986;

(j) there is—

    (i) an administrator, administrative receiver or receiver appointed in respect of it; or

    (ii) an administration order made in respect of it under schedule B1 of the Insolvency Act 1986(**f**);

(k) that person is a partnership or limited liability partnership and—

    (i) a dissolution of the partnership or limited liability partnership is ordered by any competent court, tribunal or arbitrator; or

    (ii) an event happens that makes it unlawful for the business of the partnership or limited liability partnership to continue, or for members of the partnership or limited liability partnership to carry on in partnership or limited liability partnership;

(l) the person has been—

    (i) removed under section 34 of the Charities and Trustee Investment (Scotland) Act 2005 (powers of the Court of Session)(**g**), from being concerned in the management or control of any body; or

    (ii) removed from the office of charity trustee or trustee for a charity by an order made by the Charity Commission for England and Wales or the High Court on the grounds of any misconduct or mismanagement in the administration of the charity for which the person was responsible or to which the person was privy, or which the person by the person's conduct contributed to or facilitated;

(**a**) 1995 c.46. Schedule 1 was amended by section 7(1) of the Prohibition of Female Genital Mutilation (Scotland) Act 2005 (asp 8), paragraph 2 of schedule 1 of the Protection of Children and Prevention of Sexual Offences (Scotland) Act 2005 (asp 9), paragraph 2 of schedule 5 of the Sexual Offences (Scotland) Act 2009 (asp 9) and section 41 of the Criminal Justice and Licensing (Scotland) Act 2010 (asp 13).

(**b**) 1933 c.12. Schedule 1 was amended by the paragraph 52 of schedule 4 of the Sexual Offences Act 1956 (c.69), paragraph 170(2) of schedule 16 of the Criminal Justice Act 1988 (c.33), paragraph 7 of schedule 6 of the Sexual offences Act 2003 (c.42) and paragraph 1 of schedule 5 of the Modern Slavery Act 2015 (c.3).

(**c**) 1986 c.45. Schedule 4A was inserted by section 257 and paragraph 1 of schedule 20 of the Enterprise Act 2002 (c.40) ("the 2002 Act") and was amended by paragraph 63 of the Enterprise and Regulatory Reform Act 2013 (c.24).

(**d**) 1985 c.66. Sections 56A to 56K were inserted by section 2(1) of the Bankruptcy and Diligence etc. (Scotland) Act 2007 (asp 3), amended by the Bankruptcy and Debt Advice (Scotland) Act 2014 (asp 11) and repealed by Part 1 of schedule 9 of the Bankruptcy (Scotland) Act 2016 (asp 21).

(**e**) 2016 asp 21.

(**f**) Schedule B1 was inserted by paragraph 1 of schedule 16 of the 2002 Act.

(**g**) 2005 asp 10. Section 34 was amended by section 122 of the Public Services Reform (Scotland) Act 2010 (asp 8).

(m) the person is subject to a disqualification order under section 1 of the Company Directors Disqualification Act 1986(**a**), a disqualification undertaking under section 1A of that Act, a disqualification order under article 3 of the Company Directors Disqualification (Northern Ireland) Order 2002(**b**), a disqualification undertaking under article 4 of that Order, or to an order made under section 429(2)(b) of the Insolvency Act 1986 (failure to pay under county court administration order)(**c**);

(n) the person has refused to comply with a request by the Health Board for that person to be medically examined on the grounds that the Health Board is concerned that the person is incapable of adequately providing services under the contract and, in a case where the contract is with a partnership, limited liability partnership, or a company, the Health Board is not satisfied that the contractor is taking adequate steps to deal with the matter; or

(o) the person would otherwise fall within paragraph 67(3)(e) of schedule 3 of the National Health Service (General Medical Services Contracts) Regulations 2015(**d**).

(3) A Health Board is not to terminate the contract pursuant to sub-paragraph (2)(b) where the Health Board is satisfied that the disqualification or suspension imposed by a licensing body outside the United Kingdom does not make the person unsuitable to be—

(a) a contractor;

(b) in the case of a contract with a partnership, a partner;

(c) in the case of a contract with a limited liability partnership, a member;

(d) in the case of a contract entered into on or after 22nd December 2010 with a company, as the case may be—

   (i) a member of the company; or

   (ii) a director or secretary of the company; or

(e) in the case of a contract entered into prior to 22nd December 2010 with a company limited by shares, as the case may be—

   (i) a person who legally and beneficially owns a share in that company; or

   (ii) a director or secretary of the company.

(4) A Health Board is not to terminate the contract pursuant to sub-paragraph (2)(c)—

(a) until a period of at least three months has elapsed since the date of the dismissal of the person concerned; or

(b) if, during the period of time specified in paragraph (a), the person concerned brings proceedings in any competent tribunal or court in respect of the person's dismissal, until proceedings before that tribunal or court are concluded,

and the Health Board may only terminate the contract at the end of the period specified in sub-paragraph (b) if there is no finding of unfair dismissal at the end of those proceedings.

(5) A Health Board is not to terminate the contract pursuant to sub-paragraph (2)(g)(ii) where the Health Board is satisfied that the conviction does not make the person unsuitable to be—

(a) a contractor;

(b) in the case of a contract with a partnership, a partner in that partnership;

(c) in the case of a contract with a limited liability partnership, a member of that limited liability partnership; or

---

(**a**) 1986 c.46, as relevantly amended by section 5 and paragraph 2 of schedule 4 of the Insolvency Act 2000 (c.39), section 204 of the Enterprise Act 2002 ("the 2002 Act") and paragraph 2 of schedule 7 of the Small Business, Enterprise and Employment Act 2015 (c.26) ("the 2015 Act").
(**b**) S.I. 2002/3150 (N.I. 4), as relevantly amended by paragraph 9 of schedule 8 of the 2015 Act.
(**c**) Section 429 was amended by paragraph 15 of schedule 23 of the 2002 Act.
(**d**) S.I, 2015/1862.

(d) in the case of a contract entered into prior to 22nd December 2010 with a company, as the case may be—

   (i) a person who legally and beneficially owns a share in that company; or

   (ii) a director or secretary of the company; or

(e) in the case of a contract entered into on or after 22nd December 2010 with a company, as the case may be—

   (i) a member of the company; or

   (ii) a director or secretary of the company.

(6) In this paragraph, "health service body" does not include any person who is to be regarded as a health service body in accordance with regulation 13.

Other grounds for termination by the Health Board

104. The Health Board may serve notice in writing on the contractor terminating the contract with immediate effect or with effect from such date as may be specified in the notice if—

(a) the contractor has breached the contract and, as a result of that breach, the safety of the contractor's patients is at serious risk if the contract is not terminated; or

(b) the contractor's financial situation is such that the Health Board considers that the Health Board is at risk of material financial loss.

Termination by the Health Board for unlawful sub-contracting

105. If the contractor breaches the condition specified in paragraph 62(10) and it comes to the Health Board's attention that the contractor has done so, the Health Board must serve a notice in writing on the contractor—

(a) terminating the contract with immediate effect; or

(b) instructing it to terminate the sub-contracting arrangements that give rise to the breach with immediate effect, and if it fails to comply with the instruction, the Health Board must serve a notice in writing on the contractor terminating the contract with immediate effect.

Termination by the Health Board: remedial notices and breach notices

106.—(1) Where a contractor has breached the contract other than as specified in paragraphs 101 to 105 and the breach is capable of remedy, the Health Board must, before taking any action it is otherwise entitled to take by virtue of the contract, serve a notice on the contractor requiring it to remedy the breach ("a remedial notice").

(2) A remedial notice must specify—

(a) the details of the breach;

(b) the steps the contractor must take to the satisfaction of the Health Board in order to remedy the breach; and

(c) the period during which the steps must be taken ("the notice period").

(3) The notice period must, unless the Health Board is satisfied that a shorter period is necessary to—

(a) protect the safety of the contractor's patients; or

(b) protect itself from material financial loss,

be no less than 28 days from the date that notice is given.

(4) Where a Health Board is satisfied that the contractor has not taken the required steps to remedy the breach by the end of the notice period, the Health Board may terminate the contract with effect from such date as the Health Board may specify in a further notice to the contractor.

(5) Where a contractor has breached the contract other than as specified in paragraphs 101 to 105 and the breach is not capable of remedy, the Health Board may serve notice on the contractor requiring the contractor not to repeat the breach ("breach notice").

(6) If, following a breach notice or a remedial notice, the contractor—

(a) repeats the breach that was the subject of the breach notice or the remedial notice; or

(b) otherwise breaches the contract resulting in either a remedial notice or a further breach notice,

the Health Board may serve notice on the contractor terminating the contract with effect from such date as may be specified in that notice.

(7) The Health Board is not to exercise its right to terminate the contract under sub-paragraph (6) unless it is satisfied that the cumulative effect of the breaches is such that the Health Board considers that to allow the contract to continue would be prejudicial to the efficiency of the services to be provided under the contract.

(8) If the contractor is in breach of any obligation and a breach notice or a remedial notice in respect of that default has been given to the contractor, the Health Board may withhold or deduct monies which would otherwise be payable under the contract in respect of that obligation which is the subject of the default.

Termination by the Health Board: additional provision specific to contracts with a partnership and companies limited by shares

107.—(1) Where the contractor is a company, partnership or limited liability partnership, if the Health Board becomes aware that the contractor is carrying on any business which the Health Board considers to be detrimental to the contractor's performance of its obligations under the contract—

(a) the Health Board is entitled to give notice to the contractor requiring that it ceases carrying on that business before the end of a period of not less than 28 days beginning on the day on which the notice is given ("the notice period"); and

(b) if the contractor has not satisfied the Health Board that it has ceased carrying on that business by the end of the notice period, the Health Board may, by a further written notice, terminate the contract with immediate effect or from such date as may be specified in the notice.

(2) Where the contractor is a partnership, the Health Board is entitled to terminate the contract by notice in writing on such dates as may be specified in that notice where one or more partners have left the practice during the existence of the contract if in its reasonable opinion, the Health Board considers that the change in membership of the partnership is likely to have a serious adverse impact on the ability of the contractor or the Health Board to perform its obligations under the contract.

(3) A notice given to the contractor pursuant to sub-paragraph (2) must specify—

(a) the date upon which the contract is to be terminated; and

(b) the Health Board's reasons for considering that the change in the membership of the partnership is likely to have a serious adverse impact on the ability of the contractor or the Health Board to perform its obligations under the contract.

Contract sanctions

108.—(1) In this paragraph and paragraph 109, "contract sanction" means—

(a) the termination of specified reciprocal obligations under the contract;

(b) the suspension of specified reciprocal obligations under the contract for a period of up to six months; or

(c) the withholding or deducting of monies otherwise payable under the contract.

(2) Where the Health Board is entitled to terminate the contract pursuant to paragraph 102, 103, 104, 106(4) or (6) or 107, it may instead impose any of the contract sanctions if the Health Board is reasonably satisfied that the contract sanction to be imposed is appropriate and proportionate to the circumstances giving rise to the Health Board's entitlement to terminate the contract.

(3) The Health Board is not, under sub-paragraph (2), entitled to impose any contract sanction that has the effect of terminating or suspending any obligation to provide, or any obligation that relates to, essential services.

(4) If the Health Board decides to impose a contract sanction, it must notify the contractor of the contract sanction that it proposes to impose, the date upon which that sanction will be imposed and provide in that notice an explanation of the effect of the imposition of that sanction.

(5) Subject to paragraph 109, the Health Board must not impose the contract sanction until at least 28 days after it has served notice on the contractor pursuant to sub-paragraph (4) unless the Health Board is satisfied that it is necessary to do so in order to—

    (a) protect the safety of the contractor's patients; or

    (b) protect itself from material financial loss.

(6) Where the Health Board imposes a contract sanction, the Health Board is entitled to charge the contractor the reasonable costs of additional administration that the Health Board has incurred in order to impose, or as a result of imposing, the contract sanction.

Contract sanctions and the dispute resolution procedure

109.—(1) If there is a dispute between the Health Board and the contractor in relation to a contract sanction that the Health Board is proposing to impose, the Health Board must not, subject to sub-paragraph (4), impose the proposed contract sanction except in the circumstances specified in sub-paragraph (2)(a) or (b).

(2) If the contractor refers the dispute relating to the contract sanction to the local dispute resolution process within 28 days beginning on the date on which the Health Board served notice on the contractor in accordance with paragraph 108(4) (or such longer period as may be agreed in writing with the Health Board), and notifies the Health Board in writing that it has done so, the Health Board must not impose the contract sanction unless—

    (a) there has been a resolution of the dispute between the parties which allows the Scottish Ministers to impose the contract sanction;

    (b) there has been no resolution of the dispute between the parties as a result of the local dispute resolution process and the contractor does not refer the matter to the Scottish Ministers under paragraph 91 or 92 within 28 days of the end of the period specified in—

        (i) paragraph 89(8); or

        (ii) the date on which the local dispute resolution process was completed,

    whichever is the earlier; or

    (c) either party refers the matter to the Scottish Ministers under paragraph 90 or 91 within the period specified in sub-paragraph (b) and either—

        (i) there has been a determination of the dispute pursuant to paragraph 92 and that determination permits the Health Board to impose the contract sanction; or

        (ii) the contractor ceases to pursue the NHS dispute resolution procedure.

(3) If the contractor does not invoke the NHS dispute resolution procedure within the time specified in sub-paragraph (2), the Health Board is entitled to impose the contract sanction with immediate effect.

(4) If the Health Board is satisfied that it is necessary to impose the contract sanction before the local dispute resolution process or the NHS dispute resolution procedure is concluded in order to—

    (a) protect the safety of the contractor's patients; or

    (b) protect itself from material financial loss,

the Health Board is entitled to impose the contract sanction with immediate effect, pending the outcome of that procedure.

Termination and the NHS dispute resolution procedure

110.—(1) Where the Health Board is entitled to serve written notice on the contractor terminating the contract pursuant to paragraphs 101 to 108 the Health Board must, in the notice served on the contractor pursuant to those provisions, specify a date on which the contract terminates that is not less than 28 days after the date on which the Health Board has served that notice on the contractor unless sub-paragraph (2) applies.

(2) This sub-paragraph applies if the Health Board is satisfied that a period of less than 28 days is necessary in order to—

   (a) protect the safety of the contractor's patients; or

   (b) protect itself from material financial loss.

(3) In a case falling within sub-paragraph (1), where the exceptions in sub-paragraph (2) do not apply, where the contractor invokes the local dispute resolution process before the end of the period of notice referred to in sub-paragraph (1), and it notifies the Health Board in writing that it has done so, the contract will not terminate at the end of the notice period but instead may only terminate in the circumstances specified in sub-paragraph (4).

(4) The contract may only terminate if and when—

   (a) there has been a resolution of the dispute between the parties which allows the Health Board to terminate the contract;

   (b) there has been no resolution of the dispute between the parties as a result of the local dispute resolution process and the contractor does not refer the matter to the Scottish Ministers under paragraph 91 or 92 within 28 days of the end of the period specified in—

      (i) paragraph 89(8); or

      (ii) the date on which the local dispute resolution process was completed,

      whichever is the earlier; or

   (c) either party refers the matter to the Scottish Ministers under paragraph 90 or 91 within the period specified in sub-paragraph (b) and either—

      (i) there has been a determination of the dispute pursuant to paragraph 92 and that determination permits the Health Board to terminate the contract; or

      (ii) the contractor ceases to pursue the NHS dispute resolution procedure,

whichever is the sooner.

(5) If the Health Board is satisfied that it is necessary to terminate the contract before the local dispute resolution procedure or the NHS dispute resolution procedure is concluded in order to—

   (a) protect the safety of the contractor's patients; or

   (b) protect itself from material financial loss,

sub-paragraphs (3) and (4) will not apply and the Health Board is entitled to confirm, by written notice to be served on the contractor, that the contract will nevertheless terminate at the end of the period of the notice it served pursuant to paragraphs 101 to.

Consultation with the area medical committee

111.—(1) Whenever the Health Board is considering—

   (a) terminating the contract pursuant to paragraphs 101 to 108; or

   (b) imposing a contract sanction,

it must, whenever it is reasonably practicable to do so, consult the area medical committee for its area before it terminates the contract or imposes a contract sanction.

(2) Whether or not the area medical committee has been consulted pursuant to sub-paragraph (1), whenever the Health Board imposes a contract sanction on a contractor or terminates a contract pursuant to this Part, it must, as soon as reasonably practicable, notify the area medical committee in writing of the contract sanction imposed or of the termination of the contract (as the case may be).

Where the contractor changes from being an individual to a partnership

112.—(1) If—

(a) a contractor is an individual medical practitioner who proposes to practise in partnership (but not in a limited liability partnership) ("the proposed partnership") with one or more persons ("the proposed partners");

(b) the proposed partners propose that the proposed partnership should enter into a new contract ("the new contract") with the Health Board on as similar terms as possible to the contractor's contract ("the old contract") and, as a consequence;

(c) the contractor proposes to terminate the old contract,

the contractor and the proposed partners may give written notice of those matters to the Health Board which states—

(i) the name and address of the proposed partnership and of the proposed partners;

(ii) the date on which it is proposed that the partnership should be formed and become the contractor, which must not be less than 28 days after the date of service of the notice;

(iii) that when the proposed partnership is formed, the requirements of regulations 5(2) and 6(1)(b) will be satisfied; and

(iv) whether or not the proposed partnership is to be a limited partnership and, if so, who will be a limited and who a general partner,

and the notice must be signed by the contractor and by the proposed partners as proposed partners of the proposed partnership.

(2) If the Health Board is satisfied as to the accuracy of the matters specified in the notice under sub-paragraph (1), it must give written notice to the contractor and the proposed partners that it is prepared—

(a) to terminate the old contract with effect from a specified date; and

(b) to enter into a new contract with the proposed partnership with effect from that date which is to be on the same terms as the old contract, with only such changes as are necessary to reflect the fact that the contractor will be a partnership and not an individual medical practitioner, and that the contract will have been entered into after 22nd December 2010,

and the notice must specify the changes which the Health Board considers are necessary in terms of sub-paragraph 2(b).

(3) Where it is reasonably practicable, the date specified by the Health Board in the notice under sub-paragraph (2) is to be the date proposed in the notice served under sub-paragraph (1) or, where that date is not reasonably practicable, the date specified is to be a date after that proposed date that is as close to it as is reasonably practicable.

(4) If the contractor and the proposed partners agree with what is contained in the notice by the Health Board under sub-paragraph (2)—

(a) the Health Board and the contractor are to agree in writing to terminate the old contract with effect from the date specified in that notice; and

(b) the Health Board and the partnership are to enter into a new contract with each other with effect from that date on the terms mentioned in sub-paragraph (2)(b) but subject to the changes specified in that notice.

(5) This paragraph is without prejudice to any other way in which the old contract may be terminated and a new contract entered into with the partnership.

Where the contractor changes from being a partnership to an individual

113.—(1) If a contractor is a partnership which it is proposed will be terminated or dissolved and as a consequence the contractor's contract ("the old contract") will be terminated and one of the partners wishes to enter into a new contract ("the new contract") with the Health Board as an individual medical practitioner ("the proposed contractor") on as similar terms as possible as the old contract, the partnership and the proposed contractor may give written notice thereof to the Health Board which must state—

(a) the name and address of the partnership, of the partners in that partnership and of the proposed contractor;

(b) the date on which it is proposed that the proposed contractor should become the contractor, which must not be less than 28 days after the date of service of the notice; and

(c) that the proposed contractor meets the requirements of regulations 5(1) and 6(1)(a),

and the notice must be signed by the partnership, the partners in that partnership and the proposed contractor.

(2) If the Health Board is satisfied as to the accuracy of the matters specified in the notice under sub-paragraph (1), it must give written notice to the partnership and the proposed contractor that it is prepared—

(a) to terminate the old contract with effect from a specified date; and

(b) to enter into a new contract with the proposed contractor with effect from that date which is to be on the same terms as the old contract, with only such changes as are necessary to reflect the fact that the contractor will be an individual medical practitioner and not a partnership, and that the contract will have been entered into after 22nd December 2010,

and the notice must specify the changes which the Health Board consider are necessary in terms of sub-paragraph (2)(b).

(3) Where it is reasonably practicable, the date specified by the Health Board in the notice under sub-paragraph (2) is to be the date proposed in the notice served under sub-paragraph (1) or, where that date is not reasonably practicable, the date specified is to be a date after that proposed date that is as close to it as is reasonably practicable.

(4) If the partnership and the proposed contractor agree with what is contained in the notice by the Health Board under sub-paragraph (2)—

(a) the Health Board and the partnership are to agree in writing to terminate the old contract with effect from the date specified in that notice; and

(b) the Health Board and the proposed contractor are to enter into a new contract with each other with effect from that date on the terms mentioned in sub-paragraph (2)(b) but subject to the changes specified in that notice.

(5) This paragraph is without prejudice to any other way in which the old contract may be terminated and a new contract entered into with the proposed contractor.

PART 9

MISCELLANEOUS

Clinical governance

114.—(1) The contractor must have an effective system of clinical governance.

(2) The contractor must nominate a person who will have responsibility for ensuring the effective operation of a system of clinical governance.

(3) The person nominated under sub-paragraph (2) must be a person who performs or manages services under the contract.

(4) In this paragraph "system of clinical governance" means a framework through which the contractor endeavours continuously to improve the quality of its service and safeguard high standards of care by creating an environment in which clinical excellence can flourish.

Medical Indemnity Insurance

115.—(1) The contractor must at all times have in force in relation to it an indemnity arrangement which provides appropriate cover.

(2) The contractor must not sub-contract its obligations to provide clinical services under the contract unless it has satisfied itself that the sub-contractor has in force in relation to it an indemnity arrangement which provides appropriate cover.

(3) In this paragraph—
   (a) "indemnity arrangement" means a contract of insurance or other arrangement made for the purpose of indemnifying the contractor;
   (b) "appropriate cover" means cover against liabilities that may be incurred by the contractor in the performance of clinical services under the contract, which is appropriate, having regard to the nature and extent of the risks in the performance of such services; and
   (c) a contractor is regarded as having in force in relation to it an indemnity arrangement if there is an indemnity arrangement in force in relation to a person employed or engaged by the contractor in connection with clinical services which that person provides under the contract or, as the case may be, sub-contract.

Public Liability Insurance

116. The contractor must at all times hold adequate public liability insurance in relation to liabilities to third parties arising under or in connection with the contract which are not covered by an indemnity arrangement referred to in paragraph 115.

Gifts

117.—(1) The contractor must keep a register of gifts which—
   (a) are given to any of the persons specified in sub-paragraph (2) by or on behalf of—
      (i) a patient;
      (ii) a relative of a patient; or
      (iii) any person who provides or wishes to provide services to the contractor or its patients in connection with the contract; and
   (b) have, in its reasonable opinion, an individual value of more than £100.00.

(2) The persons referred to in sub-paragraph (1) are—
   (a) the contractor;
   (b) where the contract is with a partnership, any partner;
   (c) where the contract is with a limited liability partnership, any member of the limited liability partnership;
   (d) where the contract is with a company—
      (i) any member of the company; or
      (ii) a director or secretary of the company;
   (e) any person employed by the contractor for the purposes of the contract;
   (f) any general medical practitioner engaged by the contractor for the purposes of the contract;

(g) any spouse or civil partner of a contractor (where the contractor is an individual medical practitioner) or of a person specified in paragraphs (b) to (f); or

(h) any person whose relationship with a contractor (where the contractor is an individual medical practitioner) or with a person specified in paragraphs (b) to (f) has the characteristics of the relationship between spouses or civil partners.

(3) Sub-paragraph (1) does not apply where—

(a) there are reasonable grounds for believing that the gift is unconnected with services provided or to be provided by the contractor;

(b) the contractor is not aware of the gift; or

(c) the contractor is not aware that the donor wishes to provide services to the contractor.

(4) The contractor must take reasonable steps to ensure that it is informed of gifts which fall within sub-paragraph (1) and which are given to the persons specified in sub-paragraph (2)(b) to (h).

(5) The register referred to in sub-paragraph (1) must include the following information:—

(a) the name of the donor;

(b) in a case where the donor is a patient, the patient's National Health Service number or, if the number is not known, the patient's address;

(c) in any other case, the address of the donor;

(d) the nature of the gift;

(e) the estimated value of the gift; and

(f) the name of the person or persons who received the gift.

(6) The contractor must make the register available to the Health Board on request.

Duty of candour

118. The contractor must have arrangements in place which operate in accordance with Part 2 of the Health (Tobacco, Nicotine etc. and Care) (Scotland) Act 2016(**a**), and any regulations or directions made under that part of that Act(**b**).

Compliance with legislation and guidance

119. The contractor must—

(a) comply with all relevant legislation; and

(b) have regard to all relevant guidance issued by the Health Board and the Scottish Ministers.

Third party rights

120. The contract will not create any right enforceable by any person not a party to it.

(**a**) 2016 asp 14.
(**b**) S.S.I. 2018/57.

PART 10

QUALITY

Duty to participate in quality arrangements

121.—(1) Subject to paragraph 122, the contractor must meaningfully participate in quality arrangements.

(2) The contractor must nominate a person who will be a Practice Quality Lead for the purpose of—

(a) their cluster membership; and

(b) attending meetings of the contractor's cluster.

(3) The person nominated under sub-paragraph (2) must be a general medical practitioner who performs services under the contract.

(4) In this paragraph and paragraph 122—

"cluster" means a group of practices where each practice is represented by a Practice Quality Lead;

"Cluster Quality Lead" means a person who is a member of a cluster that is appointed by a Health Board to represent that cluster to the Health Board;

"meaningfully participate" means, as a minimum—

(a) ensuring that all members of the contractor's practice supply the Practice Quality Lead with any requested information("practice quality data");

(b) considering practice quality data with the support and direction of the Practice Quality Lead; and

(c) having regard to any quality improvement measures proposed by the contractor's cluster;

"quality arrangements" means the proceedings and arrangements specified in directions given by the Scottish Ministers under section 2(5) of the Act; and

"Practice Quality Lead" means a medical practitioner nominated by a contractor to represent the contractor's practice to the cluster.

Quality arrangements

122.—(1) The contractor and the contractor's practice must comply with the quality arrangements as determined by and with the support of the Practice Quality Lead and with any further conditions relating to quality set out in directions given by Scottish Ministers under section 2(5) of the Act(**a**).

(2) The Practice Quality Lead must spend a minimum of two sessions a month in pursuance of their role and regularly attend meetings of the contractor's cluster.

(3) Where a Health Board is considering appointing a Cluster Quality Lead, that Health Board must consult a Practice Quality Lead who is a member of that cluster prior to offering an appointment.

(4) Where a cluster determines that a contractor is failing to meaningfully participate in quality arrangements it must arrange for the contractor to receive supportive measures that enable them to meet their duties under this paragraph and paragraph 121.

(**a**) Section 2(5) was amended by paragraph 19(1) of schedule 9 of the National Health Service and Community Care Act 1990 (c.19).

SCHEDULE 7
CLOSURE NOTICE

schedule 6, paragraph 26(9)

Application for List Closure

From: *Name of Contractor* To: *Name of Health Board*

Date:

In accordance with paragraph 26 of schedule 6 of the National Health Service (General Medical Services Contracts) (Scotland) Regulations 2018, on behalf of the above named contractor I/we wish to make a formal application for our list to be closed to new patients and assignments, as follows:

(1) Length of period of closure (which may not exceed 12 months and, in the absence of any agreement, will be 12 months)	
(2) Date from which closure will take effect	
(3) Date from which closure will cease to have effect	
(4) Current number of registered patients	
(5) The number of registered patients which would trigger re-opening (or suspension of list closure) of the contractor's list of patients, expressed either or a number of registered patients or as a percentage of the number indicated in (4)	
(6) The number of registered patients which would trigger a re-closure (or lifting of the suspension of list closure) of the list, expressed either as a number of registered patients or as a percentage of the number indicated in (4)	
(7) Any withdrawal or reduction of additional or enhanced services	

Signed ....

For [Name of contractor]

SCHEDULE 8

schedule 6, paragraph 74

INFORMATION TO BE INCLUDED IN PRACTICE LEAFLETS

A practice leaflet must include—

1. The name of the contractor.

2. In the case of a contract with a partnership—

(a) whether or not it is a limited partnership; and

(b) the names of all the partners and, in the case of a limited partnership, their status as a general or limited partner.

3. In the case of a contract with a company—

(a) the names of the directors, the company secretary and the members of that company; and

(b) the address of the company's registered office.

4. In the case of a contract with a limited liability partnership—

(a) the names of all the members; and

(b) the address of the registered office of the limited liability partnership.

5. The full name of each person performing services under the contract.

6. In the case of each health care professional performing services under the contract the health care professional's professional qualifications.

7. Whether the contractor undertakes the teaching or training of health care professionals or persons intending to become health care professionals.

8. The contractor's practice area, by reference to a map, plan or postcode.

9. The address of each of the practice premises.

10. The contractor's telephone number and the address of the contractor's website (if any).

11. Where the contractor offers its registered patients an online service in accordance with paragraph 72 of schedule 6, the website address where such patients can access and use the service and guidance on how such patients can access and use that service.

12. Whether the practice premises have suitable access for all disabled patients and, if not, the alternative arrangements for providing services to such patients.

13. How to register as a patient.

14. The right of patients to express a preference of practitioner in accordance with paragraph 15 of Schedule 6 and the means of expressing such a preference.

15. The services available under the contract.

16. The opening hours of the practice premises and the method of obtaining access to services throughout the core hours. Information on access to services should include any usual periods of consultation time provided during the opening hours.

17. The criteria for home visits and the method of obtaining such a visit.

18.—(1) Details of—

(a) the out of hours period as set out in sub-paragraph (2);

(b) the arrangements for services in the out of hours period; and

(c) how the patient may contact such services.

(2) The out of hours period is—

(a) the period beginning at 1830 hours on any day from Monday to Thursday and ending at 0800 hours on the following day;

(b) the period beginning 1830 hours on Friday and ending at 0800 hours on the following Monday; and

(c) Christmas Day, New Year's Day and any other public or local holiday.

19. If the services in paragraph 18 are not provided by the contractor, the fact that the Health Board referred to in paragraph 27 is responsible for commissioning the services.

20. The telephone number of NHS 24 and details of the NHS 24 website.

21. The method by which patients are to obtain repeat prescriptions.

22. If the contractor is a dispensing contractor the arrangements for dispensing prescriptions.

23. How patients may make a complaint or comment on the provision of service.

24. The rights and responsibilities of the patient, including keeping appointments.

25. The action that may be taken where a patient is violent or abusive to the contractor, the contractor's staff, persons present on the practice premises or in the place where treatment is provided under the contract or other persons specified in paragraph 18(2) of Schedule 6.

26. Details of who has access to patient information (including information from which the identity of the individual can be ascertained) and the patient's rights in relation to disclosure of such information.

27. The name, address and telephone number of the Health Board which is a party to the contract and from whom details of primary medical services in the area may be obtained.

SCHEDULE 9

Regulation 34

REVOCATIONS

Column 1 *Secondary legislation revoked*	Column 2 *Reference*	Column 3 *Extent of revocation*
The National Health Service (General Medical Services Contracts) (Scotland) Regulations 2004	S.S.I. 2004/115	The whole Regulations, subject to regulation 33(1) and paragraph 2 of schedule 6 of these Regulations
The General Medical Services (Transitional and Other Ancillary Provisions) (Scotland) Order 2004	S.S.I. 2004/142	The whole Regulations
The Primary Medical Services (Sale of Goodwill and Restrictions on Sub-contracting) (Scotland) Regulations 2004	S.S.I. 2004/162	Regulation 4
The National Health Service (General Medical Services (Contracts) (Scotland) Amendment Regulations 2004	S.S.I. 2004/215	The whole Regulations
The National Health Service (General Medical Services Contracts) (Scotland) Amendment Regulations 2005	S.S.I. 2005/337	The whole Regulations, subject to regulation 33(3) and schedule 6, paragraph 2 of these Regulations
The National Health Service (General Medical Services Contracts) (Scotland) Amendment Regulations 2006	S.S.I. 2006/247	The whole Regulations
The National Health Service (General Medical Services Contracts) (Scotland) Amendment Regulations 2007	S.S.I. 2007/206	The whole Regulations
The National Health Service (General Medical Services Contracts) (Scotland) Amendment (No. 2) Regulations 2007	S.S.I. 2007/392	The whole Regulations
The National Health Service (General Medical Services Contracts) (Scotland) Amendment (No. 3) Regulations 2007	S.S.I. 2007/501	The whole Regulations
The National Health Service (Pharmaceutical Services) (Scotland) Regulations 2009	S.S.I. 2009/183	Schedule 6, paragraph 4

The National Health Service (General Medical Services Contracts, Primary Medical Services Section 17C Agreements and Primary Medical Services Performers Lists) (Scotland) Amendment Regulations 2010	S.S.I. 2010/93	Regulation 2
The National Health Service (General Medical Services Contracts) (Scotland) Amendment Regulations 2010	S.S.I. 2010/394	The whole Regulations
National Health Service (Pharmaceutical Services) (Scotland) Amendment Regulations 2011	S.S.I. 2011/32	The words "under the terms of a general medical services contract" to "the National Health Service (General Medical Services Contracts) (Scotland) Regulations 2004" in regulation 3
The National Health Service (Free Prescriptions and Charges for Drugs and Appliances) (Scotland) Regulations 2011	S.S.I. 2011/55	Schedule 1, paragraph 4
Public Services Reform (Scotland) Act 2010 (Consequential Modifications) Order 2011	S.S.I. 2011/211	Schedule 1, paragraph 31 and schedule 2, paragraph 25, subject to regulation 33(3) of these Regulations
The National Health Service (General Medical Services Contracts) (Scotland) Amendment Regulations 2012	S.S.I. 2012/9	The whole Regulations
The Patient Rights (Complaints Procedure and Consequential Provisions) (Scotland) Regulations 2012	S.S.I. 2012/36	Schedule 1, paragraph 1
The National Health Service (Physiotherapist, Podiatrist or Chiropodist Independent Prescribers) (Miscellaneous Amendments) (Scotland) Regulations 2014	S.S.I. 2014/73	Regulations 2, 3 and 4
The National Health Service (Pharmaceutical Services) (Scotland) (Miscellaneous Amendments) Regulations 2014	S.S.I. 2014/148	Regulations 10 and 11
The National Health Service (Dietitian Supplementary Prescribers and Therapeutic Radiographer Independent Prescribers) (Miscellaneous Amendments) (Scotland) Regulations 2016	S.S.I. 2016/393	Regulations 2, 3 and 4

SCHEDULE 10

Regulation 35

CONSEQUENTIAL AMENDMENTS

The National Health Service (Scotland) (Injury Benefits) Regulations 1998

1.—(1) The National Health Service (Scotland) (Injury Benefits) Regulations 1998(**a**) are amended as follows.

(2) In regulation 2 (interpretation), in the definition of "enhanced services"(**b**), for "regulation 2(1) of the National Health Service (General Medical Services Contracts) (Scotland) Regulations 2004" substitute "regulation 3(1) of the National Health Service (General Medical Services Contracts) (Scotland) Regulations 2018".

The National Health Service (Primary Medical Services Performers Lists) (Scotland) Regulations 2004

2.—(1) The National Health Service (Primary Medical Services Performers Lists (Scotland) Regulations 2004(**c**) are amended as follows.

(2) In regulation 2 (interpretation), in the definition of "General Medical Services Contracts Regulations", for "the National Health Service (General Medical Services Contracts) (Scotland) Regulations 2004" substitute "the National Health Service (General Medical Services Contracts) (Scotland) Regulations 2018".

(3) In schedule 1—

(a) in paragraph 3(c)(i), for "paragraph 114 (gifts) of Schedule 5 to" substitute "paragraph 117 (gifts) of schedule 6 of"; and

(b) in paragraph 3(d)(i), for "paragraph 114 of Schedule 5 to" substitute "paragraph 117 (gifts) of schedule 6 of".

The Primary Medical Services (Sale of Goodwill and Restrictions on Sub-contracting) (Scotland) Regulations 2004

3.—(1) The Primary Medical Services (Sale of Goodwill and Restrictions on Sub-contracting) (Scotland) Regulations 2004(**d**) are amended as follows.

(2) In regulation 2(1) (interpretation)—

(a) in the definition of "enhanced services", in both places it appears, for "2(1)" substitute "3(1)";

(b) in the definition of "essential services", for "15(3), (5), (6) and (8)" substitute "18(3), (5), (6) and (8)"; and

(c) in the definition of "GMS Contracts Regulations", for "the National Health Service (General Medical Services Contracts) (Scotland) Regulations 2004" substitute "the National Health Service (General Medical Services Contracts) (Scotland) Regulations 2018".

(**a**) S.S.I. 1998/1594 as relevantly amended by S.S.I. 2005/512.
(**b**) The definition of "enhanced services" was amended by S.S.I. 2005/512.
(**c**) S.S.I. 2004/114.
(**d**) S.S.I. 2004/162.

The General Medical Services and Section 17C Agreements (Transitional and other Ancillary Provisions) (Scotland) Order 2004

4.—(1) The General Medical Services and Section 17C Agreements (Transitional and other Ancillary Provisions) (Scotland) Order 2004(**a**) are amended as follows.

(2) In article 1(2) (interpretation)—

(a) omit the definition of "the 2004 Regulations";

(b) insert the following definition at the appropriate place—

""the GMS Contracts Regulations" means the National Health Service (General Medical Services Contracts) (Scotland) Regulations 2018;";

(c) in the definition of "list of patients", in paragraph (b), for "paragraph 14 of Schedule 5 to" substitute "paragraph 11 of schedule 6 of";

(d) in the definition of "practice premises", for the second "regulation 2(1)" substitute "regulation 3(1)"; and

(e) in the definition of "temporary resident", for "paragraph 16 of Schedule 5 to" substitute "paragraph 13 of schedule 6 of".

(3) In article 3(a) (applications for inclusion in list of patients), for "paragraph 15 of Schedule 5 to" substitute "paragraph 12 of schedule 6 of".

(4) In article 4 (acceptance of applications for inclusion in lists of patients)(**b**)—

(a) in paragraph (a), for "paragraph 15(5) of Schedule 5 to" substitute "paragraph 12(5) of schedule 6 of"; and

(b) omit paragraph (2).

(5) In article 5(a) (removal from the list of patients at the request of the patient)—

(a) for "paragraph 19 of Schedule 5 to" substitute "paragraph 16 of schedule 6 of"; and

(b) for "19(3)(b)" substitute "16(3)(b)".

(6) In article 6(2)(a) (removal from the list of patients at the request of the relevant medical practitioner), for "paragraph 20(8) of Schedule 5 to" substitute "paragraph 17(8) of schedule 6 of".

(7) In article 8(a) (removals from the list of patients who have moved)—

(a) for "paragraph 24 of Schedule 5 to" substitute "paragraph 21 of schedule 6 of"; and

(b) for "paragraph 24(a)" substitute "paragraph 21(a)".

(8) In article 10(a) (applications for acceptance as a temporary resident) for "paragraphs 16 and 17 of Schedule 5 to" substitute "paragraphs 13 and 14 of schedule 6 of".

(9) In article 11(2)(a) (acceptance of temporary residents), for "paragraph 16 of Schedule 5 to" substitute "paragraph 13 of schedule 6 of".

(10) In article 14(3)(a) (newly registered patients), for "paragraph 4 of Schedule 5 to" substitute "paragraph 5 of schedule 6 of".

(11) In article 15 (appointments system), for paragraph 74(c) of Schedule 5 to" substitute "paragraph 78(c) of schedule 6 of".

(12) In article 18(1)(a) (patient records), for "paragraph 66 of Schedule 5 to" substitute "paragraph 68 of schedule 6 of".

(13) In article 19(1)(a) (rights of entry), for "paragraph 81 of Schedule 5 to" substitute "paragraph 86 of schedule 6 of".

(14) In article 22(a) (complaints relating to general medical services made after 31st March 2004), for "paragraph 82 of Schedule 5 to" substitute "paragraph 87 of schedule 6 of".

(**a**) S.S.I. 2004/163.
(**b**) Article 4(1) was amended by S.S.I. 2004/223.

(15) In article 23(1)(a) (reports to a medical officer), for "paragraph 72 of Schedule 5 to" substitute "paragraph 76 of schedule 6 of".

(16) In article 24 (arrangements with organisations providing deputy doctors)—

    (a) in paragraph (1)(**a**), for "paragraph 103(1) of Schedule 5 to" substitute "paragraph 106(1) of schedule 6 of";

    (b) in paragraph (2), for "paragraph 103(6) of Schedule 5 to" substitute "paragraph 106(6) of schedule 6"; and

    (c) in paragraph (3), for "paragraph 103(1) of Schedule 5 to" substitute "paragraph 106(1) of schedule 6 of".

(17) In article 25(4)(b) (practice leaflet), for "regulation 2(1)" substitute "regulation 3(1)".

(18) In article 29(2) (arrangements for GP registrars), for "regulation 2(1)" substitute "regulation 3(1)".

(19) In article 35(1) (carry over of approvals, applications, notices etc.)—

    (a) in sub-paragraph (j), for "paragraph 18 of Schedule 5 to" substitute "paragraph 15 of schedule 6 of";

    (b) in sub-paragraph (l), for "paragraphs 66(6) or 79(1) or (3) of Schedule 5 to" substitute "paragraphs 68(5), or 84(1) or (3) of schedule 6 of"; and

    (c) in sub-paragraph (m), for "paragraph 20(3) of Schedule 5 to" substitute "paragraph 17(3) of schedule 6 of".

(20) In article 36 (newly registered patients)—

    (a) in paragraph (1), in both places it appears, for "paragraph 4 of Schedule 5 to" substitute "paragraph 5 of schedule 6 of"; and

    (b) in paragraph (2), for "paragraph 4(2) of Schedule 5 to" substitute "paragraph 5(2) of schedule 6 of".

(21) In article 37 (temporary residents), in both places it appears, for "paragraph 16 of Schedule 5 to" substitute "paragraph 13 of schedule 6 of".

(22) In article 38 (provision of immediately necessary treatment), for "regulation 15" substitute "regulation 18".

(23) In article 39 (removals from the list of patients)—

    (a) in paragraph (1), for "paragraph 19(3) of Schedule 5 to" substitute "paragraph 16(3) of schedule 6 of";

    (b) in paragraph (2), in both places it appears, for "paragraph 23 of Schedule 5 to" substitute "paragraph 20 of schedule 6 of"; and

    (c) in paragraph (3), in both places it appears, for "paragraph 24 of Schedule 5 to" substitute "paragraph 21 of schedule 6 of".

(24) In article 40 (requirement to provide dispensing services)—

    (a) in paragraph (1), for "Schedule 5 to" substituted "schedule 6 of"; and

    (b) in paragraph (2), for "regulation 2(1) substitute "regulation 3(1)".

(25) In article 42 (complaints)—

    (a) in paragraph (1), in both places it appears, for "paragraph 82 of Schedule 5 to" substitute "paragraph 87 of schedule 6 of"; and

    (b) in paragraph (2), for "paragraphs 82 to 86 and 88 of Schedule 5 to" substitute "paragraph 88 of schedule 6".

(26) In article 43(1) (refund of fees)—

    (a) for "regulation 24(3)" substitute "regulation 28(3)"; and

---

(**a**) Article 24(1) was amended by S.S.I. 2004/223.

(b) for "regulation 24(4)" substitute "regulation 28(4)".

(27) In article 44(1)(a) (annual returns and reviews), for "paragraph 73 of Schedule 5 to" substitute "paragraph 77 of schedule 6 of".

(28) In article 46 (grounds for termination of the general medical services contract), in both places it appears, for "paragraph 101 of Schedule 5 to" substitute "paragraph 103 of schedule 6 of".

(29) Omit Part 6.

(30) Insert after Article 61—

"PART 6A

APPLICATION OF THE NATIONAL HEALTH SERVICE (GENERAL MEDICAL SERVICES) (SCOTLAND) REGULATIONS 2018

Provision of out of hours services

62A. Regulation 33 of the GMS Contracts Regulations shall apply to all contracts, including default contracts, to which Part 6 of this Order applied on 31st March 2018, as if these contracts were contracts which included a requirement to provide out of hours services pursuant to regulation 32 of the National Health Service (General Medical Services Contracts) (Scotland) Regulations 2004(**a**) on 31st March 2018. ".

(31) In article 79(3) (determination of a Health Board or the Scottish Ministers made before the relevant date), for "paragraph 103(7) of Schedule 5 to" substitute "paragraph 106(7) of schedule 6 of".

(32) In article 80(5) (determination of a Health Board made on or after the relevant date), for "paragraph 103(7) of Schedule 5 to" substitute "paragraph 106(7) of schedule 6 of".

(33) In article 81(8) (appeals to the Scottish Ministers against determinations of Health Boards), for paragraph 103(7) of Schedule 5 to" substitute "paragraph 106(7) of schedule 6 of".

(34) Wherever it appears in the Order, for "the 2004 Regulations" substitute "the GMS Contract Regulations".

(35) In articles 16, 17(**b**), 29(1)(a), 35(1)(k) and (2), 41(1) and 45(2), wherever it appears, for "Schedule 5 to" substitute "schedule 6 of".

The National Health Service (Pharmaceutical Services) (Scotland) Regulations 2009

5.—(1) The National Health Service (Pharmaceutical Services) (Scotland) Regulations 2009(**c**) are amended as follows.

(2) In regulation 2 (interpretation and application)—

   (a) in paragraph (b) of the definition of "appropriate non-proprietary name", for "Schedule 5 to" substitute "schedule 6 of ";

   (b) in paragraph (a) of the definition of "dispensing doctor"(**d**), for "paragraph 44 of Schedule 5 to the National Health Service (General Medical Services Contracts) (Scotland) Regulations 2004" substitute "paragraph 44 of schedule 6 of the GMS Contracts Regulations";

   (c) in the definition of "GMS Contracts Regulations", for "the National Health Service (General Medical Services Contracts) (Scotland) Regulations 2004" substitute "the

---

(**a**) S.S.I. 2004/115.
(**b**) Article 17 was amended by S.S.I. 2004/223.
(**c**) S.S.I. 2009/183.
(**d**) The definition of dispensing doctor was inserted by S.S.I. 2011/32

National Health Service (General Medical Services Contracts) (Scotland) Regulations 2018"; and

(d) in paragraph (b) of the definition of "scheduled drug", for "Schedule 5 to" substitute "schedule 6 of".

The National Health Service Superannuation Scheme (Scotland) Regulations 2011

6.—(1) The National Health Service Superannuation Scheme (Scotland) Regulations 2011(**a**) are amended as follows.

(2) In regulation A2(4) (interpretation)—

(a) in paragraph (a) of the definition of "additional services", for "Schedule 1 to the National Health Service (General Medical Services Contracts) (Scotland) Regulations 2004" substitute "schedule 1 of the National Health Service (General Medical Services Contracts) (Scotland) Regulations 2018";

(b) in the definition of "certification services", for "Schedule 3 to the National Health Service (General Medical Services Contracts) (Scotland) Regulations 2004" substitute "schedule 4 of the National Health Service (General Medical Services Contracts) (Scotland) Regulations 2018";

(c) in the definition of "enhanced services", in both places it appears, for "regulation 2(1) of the National Health Service (General Medical Services Contracts) (Scotland) Regulations 2004" substitute "regulation 3(1) of the National Health Service (General Medical Services Contracts) (Scotland) Regulations 2018"; and

(d) in the definition of "essential services", for "regulation 15 of the National Health Service (General Medical Services Contracts) (Scotland) Regulations 2004" substitute "regulation 18 of the National Health Service (General Medical Services Contracts) (Scotland) Regulations 2018".

The Patient Rights (Complaints Procedure and Consequential Provisions) (Scotland) Regulations 2012

7.—(1) The Patient Rights (Complaints Procedure and Consequential Provisions) (Scotland) Regulations 2012(**b**) are amended as follows.

(2) In regulation 1(2) (citation, commencement and interpretation), for sub-paragraph (i) of the definition of "relevant complaints procedure", substitute—

"(i) part 6 of schedule 6 of the National Health Service (General Medical Services Contracts) (Scotland) Regulations 2018;".

The National Health Service Superannuation Scheme (2008 Section) (Scotland) Regulations 2013

8.—(1) The National Health Service Superannuation Scheme (2008 Section) (Scotland) Regulations 2013(**c**) are amended as follows.

(2) In regulation 2.A.1 (interpretation of Part 2: general)—

(a) omit the definition of "the 2004 Regulations"; and

(b) insert the following definition at the appropriate place—

""the GMS Contracts Regulations" means the National Health Service (General Medical Services Contracts) (Scotland) Regulations 2018;";

(c) for "the 2004 Regulations", wherever they occur, substitute "the GMS Contracts Regulations"; and

---

(**a**) S.S.I. 2011/117.
(**b**) S.S.I. 2012/36.
(**c**) S.S.I. 2013/174.

(d) in the definition of "certification services", for "Schedule 3 (list of prescribed medical certificates) to" substitute "schedule 4 (list of prescribed medical certificates) of".

(3) In regulation 3.A.1 (interpretation of Part 3: general)—

(a) omit the definition of "the 2004 Regulations";

(b) insert the following definition at the appropriate place—

""the GMS Contracts Regulations" means the National Health Service (General Medical Services Contracts) (Scotland) Regulations 2018;";

(c) for "the 2004 Regulations", wherever they occur,, substitute "the GMS Contracts Regulations"; and

(d) in the definition of "certification services", for "Schedule 3 (list of prescribed medical certificates) to" substitute "schedule 4 (list of prescribed medical certificates) of";

(e) in the definition of "enhanced services", in both places it appears, for "2(1)" substitute "3(1)"; and

(f) in the definition of "essential services", for "15" substitute "18".

The Public Bodies (Joint Working) (Prescribed Health Board Functions) (Scotland) Regulations 2014

9.—(1) The Public Bodies (Joint Working) (Prescribed Health Board Functions) (Scotland) Regulations 2014(**a**) are amended as follows.

(2) In paragraph 1 of schedule 3 (interpretation of schedule 3), in the definition of "out of hours period", for "regulation 2 of the National Health Service (General Medical Services Contracts) (Scotland) Regulations 2004" substitute "regulation 3 of the National Health Service (General Medical Services Contracts) (Scotland) Regulations 2018".

National Health Service Pension Scheme (Scotland) Regulations 2015

10.—(1) The National Health Service Pension Scheme (Scotland) Regulations 2015(**b**) are amended as follows.

(2) In paragraph 2(2) of schedule 8, in paragraph (i) of CASE 1, for "the 2004 Regulations" substitute "the GMS Contracts Regulations".

(3) In schedule 13 (Definitions)—

(a) omit the definition of "the 2004 Regulations";

(b) insert the following definition at the appropriate place—

""the GMS Contracts Regulations" means the National Health Service (General Medical Services Contracts) (Scotland) Regulations 2018";

(c) for "the 2004 Regulations", wherever they occur, substitute "the GMS Contracts Regulations";

(d) in the definition of "certification services", for "Schedule 3 to" substitute "schedule 4 of";

(e) in the definition of "enhanced services", for "2(1)" substitute "3(1)"; and

(f) in the definition of "essential services", for "15" substitute "18".

(**a**) S.S.I. 2014/344.
(**b**) S.S.I. 2015/94.

EXPLANATORY NOTE

(This note is not part of the Regulations)

These Regulations consolidate the National Health Service (General Medical Services Contracts) Regulations 2004 and set out, for Scotland, the framework for general medical services contracts under section 17J of the National Health Service (Scotland) Act 1978 ("the Act").

Part 2 of the Regulations prescribes the conditions which, in accordance with section 17L(1) of the Act, must be met by a contractor before the Health Board may enter into a general medical services contract with it.

Part 3 of the Regulations prescribes the procedure for pre-contract dispute resolution, in accordance with section 17O(1) of the Act.

Part 4 of the Regulations sets out the procedures, in accordance with section 17O(2) of the Act, by which a contractor may elect to be regarded as a health service body for any purposes of section 17A of the Act and modifies section 17A in relation to such a person.

Part 5 of (and schedules 1 to 6, 7 and 8 to) the Regulations prescribe the terms which, in accordance with sections 17K and 17N of the Act, must be included in a general medical services contract (in addition to those contained in the Act).

The prescribed terms include terms relating to—

(a) the type and duration of the contract (regulations 14 to 17);

(b) the services to be provided (regulations 18, 19 and 21 to 23 and schedule 1), the manner in which they are to be provided (Part 1 of schedule 6) and the procedures for opting out of additional (regulation 20 and schedule 2);

(c) the issuing of medical certificates (regulation 25 and schedule 4);

(d) finance, fees and charges (regulations 26 to 28 and schedule 5);

(e) patient registration and removal, lists closures and assignments (schedule 6, Part 2 and schedule 7);

(f) prescribing and dispensing (schedule 6, Part 3);

(g) the conditions to be met by those who perform services or are employed or engaged by the contractor (schedule 6, Part 4);

(h) patient records, the provision of information and rights of entry (schedule 6, Part 5 and schedule 8);

(i) complaints (schedule 6, Part 6);

(j) procedures for dispute resolution (schedule 6, Part 7); and

(k) procedures for variation and termination of contracts (schedule 6, Part 8).

Part 6 of the Regulations prescribes functions for area medical committees.

Part 7 of the Regulations makes transitional provision for persons continuing to provide out of hours services, notwithstanding the repeal of the National Health Service (Primary Medical Services Section 17C Agreements)(Scotland) Regulations 2004.

Part 8 of (and schedules 9 and 10 to) the Regulations amends or revokes provisions of existing legislation in consequence of the making of these Regulations.

© Crown copyright 2018

Printed and published in the UK by The Stationery Office Limited under the authority and superintendence of Jeff James, the Queen's Printer for Scotland.